BUILDINGS
of
EARTH
and
STRAW

*In the beginner's mind there are many possibilities;
in the expert's mind there are few . . .*

*This is the real secret of the arts:
always be a beginner.*

— Shunryu Suzuki
Zen Mind, Beginner's Mind

BUILDINGS

of

EARTH

and

STRAW

Structural Design for Rammed Earth
and Straw-bale Architecture

Bruce King, P. E.

ECOLOGICAL DESIGN PRESS
1996

Ecological Design Press is a project of the non-profit Ecological Design Institute (EDI). EDI's mission is to achieve a better fit between the human and natural environments through ecological design education and research. EDI's affiliate, the Van der Ryn Design Group, specializes in earth, straw, and environmentally friendly building.

Correspondence for the author may be addressed to him care of the publisher:

Ecological Design Press
245 Gate Five Road
Sausalito, California 94965
ecodes@aol.com
www.ecodesign.org/edi

Additional copies of this book may be ordered from the distributor:

Chelsea Green Publishing Company
P.O. Box 428
White River Junction, Vermont 05001
800-639-4099

All illustrations are by the author unless noted otherwise.

Printed in the United States of America.
00 99 98   2 3 4 5

Library of Congress Cataloging-in-Publication Data is available upon request.

ISBN # 0-9644718-1-7

For Mom and Dad, of course,
and for Seymour's Fat Lady

and for the children

FOREWORD

Bruce King has produced a book that is both long overdue and quite timely. The depletion of our forests and the awakening to the need for sustainable growth practices has brought about considerable interest in building with earth and straw as a way of reducing our reliance on wood. While we have known examples of earth and straw construction dating back hundreds of years, our technical society demands facts relating to the materials we use for building purposes. Building codes allow local officials to approve alternate materials and methods of construction provided they meet prescribed standards in the code for strength, effectiveness, fire resistance, durability, safety, and sanitation. However, it has been very difficult to find the information required by building departments to approve construction with earth and straw. Bruce has provided that information in this book.

I own a ranch in Texas where I raise cattle, along with crops of wheat and hay. A by-product of harvesting wheat is straw, and there have been times when I've had to burn my straw in order to retill the land after harvest. This same process occurs in the Sacramento Valley of California after rice is harvested, and when I see the sky turn brown from the burning of the rice fields, I think, "What a shame it is to be wasting such a wonderful construction material." An elegant solution to the farmer's disposal problem is to bale the straw and sell it to builders. The result could be decent, safe, and sanitary housing for a society that frequently provides substandard or inadequate housing for many of its citizens. As a city official, I am heartened by the possibilities presented in such an ecologically sound and socially evolved idea.

I have a very special regard for those who show independence in their thinking — true entrepreneurs and born survivors. When I talk to people interested in building with alternate materials, I find that a great majority fall into this category. There are no large manufacturing companies willing to do the research and development on these materials because very few can get patents or otherwise claim proprietary rights to the results. Bruce has donated a tremendous amount of his time and his considerable engineering skill toward supplying those of us in need of this book with a concise, understandable, and well-written text. While I find most technical books to be dry, uninteresting, and difficult to read, Bruce has managed to provide technical information in an accessible and entertaining manner. Although parts of his book will admittedly require engineering training to understand, even the uninitiated builder will find a wealth of usable material here.

Bob Fowler, F.A.I.A., P.E., P.B.O.;
past chairman, International Conference of Building Officials;
founding member, International Codes Council

TABLE OF CONTENTS

This book is intended for two very different types of people —
technical folks (engineers, building officials, architects) and
normal folks (primarily homeowners). This means that some of
the information is going to be very useful to some of you and
not so useful to the rest of you. Without sacrificing clarity or
thoroughness, every effort has been made to juggle the infor-
mation needs of both sets of people.

LIST OF FIGURES

PREFACE

This book is an attempt to gather together, organize, and digest all that has been learned about the use of earth and straw as building structures, a broad review as much as a textbook or manual. Our knowledge to date is somewhat anecdotal and still evolving, and as such I am enormously indebted to the many individuals who, besides having pioneered these old/new technologies, were more than generous in assisting my research.

Particular thanks go to those who gave of time they could hardly spare to review the text at various stages: David Easton, Matts Myhrman, Judy Knox, David Eisenberg, Dan Smith, Kelly Lerner, Bob Theis, John "Balehead" Swearingen, David Randolph, Scott Parker, and Fred Webster. To say that these people helped would be a gross understatement, for this book could never pretend to be thorough, nor have been such a pleasure to research, without their immeasurable support and contributions. Although they were kind enough to review content and correct inaccuracies, any mistakes that may remain are entirely my own.

Further embellishment and refinement came out of conversations with Herman Bojarsky, Tony Perry, Ed Paschich, David Bainbridge, Rick Green, Karl Bareis, Tom Luecke, Cynthia Wright, Greg McMillan, Turko Semmes, Janet Johnston, Robert Glassco, David Arkin, Polly Cooper, Ken Haggard, Leonard Opel, Bob Foster, Kim Thompson, Pete Retondo, Ross Burkhardt, James Kalin, Bill and Athena Steen, Michael Forbes, Dennis Fagent, Greg Van Mechelen, Jeff Oldham, and Long Tall Rob Tom; my thanks and appreciation to each of you.

In addition to a few of the above, thanks go to many who helped in the effort without necessarily knowing they were doing so: Tom Casadevall of the U.S. Geological Survey, who explained why Missouri has earthquakes; my sister-in-law, Ann-Marie Weller, for the engineer joke; Moe Dog, for endless, cheerful technical support; Pete Gang, who delicately suggested that there be "lots of pictures"; David Arkin, Dan Smith, and Bob Theis for lots of pictures; and Lancé Wyeth, who started it all with a heated dissertation on foreign policy.

Final thanks go to my publisher, client, and friend, Sim Van der Ryn, granddaddy of ecological design, who for decades has been pointing to new possibilities in the built environment; Michael Klein, for his generous support of stabilized earth research; my editor, Ann Edminster, who deftly molded my literary spasms into a coherent presentation; Marci Riseman, who kept the ball rolling; Anne Hayes, for the excruciating work of proofreader; Janet Hekking, for an inspired cover design; and my wife, Sarah, for helping in a thousand ways and enduring temporary widowhood so uncomplainingly.

Here, reader, is what I could gather together about earth and straw — a sketchy, inaugural engineering essay that perhaps raises as many questions as it answers. It may also generate some frustration: engineers may bemoan the relative paucity of firm information that is available while, at the other end of the spectrum, owner-builders may recoil in horror at the appearance of the plodding, heavy-handed engineering approach to what have heretofore been as much art forms as building systems. As the years go by, I hope and trust that others will join in the effort to develop and refine our understanding of these ubiquitous materials, easing their acceptance into the builder's palette. I have no doubt that earth and straw architecture will play an ever-greater role in providing shelter for all people in the coming millennium.

Bruce King
Fall, 1996
Sausalito, California

Introduction

Ignorance is not not knowin' —
Ignorance is knowin' what ain't so.

— Mark Twain

Sure, sure, we've all heard the story of the three little pigs. The big, bad wolf comes along and blows down the first pig's house, a house of straw, and eats the pig. Then he huffs and puffs and blows down the second pig's house, a house of sticks, and eats that pig. Then he comes to the third pig's brick house, and he blows and he blows but he can't blow it down.

That's what they tell you. What they don't tell you — what came out later in the ensuing litigation — is that the wolf was both smart and patient. He lay down to have a nice nap, and eventually an earthquake jolted through, reducing the brick house to rubble. And he ate the third pig. The lesson? No single material is perfect for every house, or is perfect at all. The smart builder will review his or her own dreams, needs, limitations, available resources, site, climate, wolves — everything — and then design the house that best fits all of those things, unhindered by any impulse to simply build the way everyone else is building.

Of course, the real moral of the story is, as Matts Myhrman tells us:

"Don't let a pig build your house!"

What's the best way to build a house? How would you build a house without using wood? How would you build a house that won't burn? How would you build a house with the least impact on the environment? How would you build the best house for yourself, for your family, for your community?

In seeking the answer to these and other questions, many people have begun to rediscover old ways of building and to experiment with new forms using old techniques. They are building lovely, comfortable, durable buildings from two substances that are around us almost everywhere: earth and straw. Somewhat out of sight of the mainstream architecture and construction communities, people are putting up new projects every day and talking to each other about problems encountered, problems solved, and the pleasures of discovery and invention; it could almost be called a movement. If so, however, it is a movement with only sketchy organization and hazy definition. As, perhaps, with any other trend, it appears different from different perspectives.

An architect might speak of "ecological design" or "sustainable design," referring to the dawning awareness that we in construction (as well as other domains of modern, industrialized life) are consuming resources far faster than we are replenishing them (or letting them replenish themselves). Sustainable design, then, looks to find ways to build that can be continued for an indefinite number of generations to come and to make clever use of at least some of the torrent of waste products that surround us. The ash produced by coal-burning power plants is now used to make high-grade concrete; wood chips and scraps at the lumber mill, formerly just trash, are now pressed into useful waferboard; and plastic is being recycled and remolded into strong, durable "lumber." The earth excavated from a site can become the walls of a new building. And the straw left over from the grain harvest, formerly burned (producing stupendous amounts of carbon dioxide and particulate pollution) can be baled and turned into warm, inexpensive houses. The grass that surrounds you and the earth underfoot can become the walls of your home.

Owner-builders — who may have some property and simply want to build a house — might also be interested in ecological design. They also might not. They (you?) might simply want a building that won't burn because it will be far from any fire department and surrounded by flammable chaparral. Or you might have seen some pictures of rammed earth and want your house, too, to look as if it were carved from a piece of the Grand Canyon. Or you were once in a straw-bale house and were charmed by the rounded edges, undulating lines, and indescribable quiet and warmth. Or you might just want something inexpensive that you can build yourself and that won't require much heating or cooling.

An engineer or building inspector, however, might recoil nervously from one of these building techniques because it's Not-What-I-Know and Not-What-We-Do-Around-Here. In the eyes of the building codes, what we are talking about is not, per se, ecological, charming, or Grand Canyonish; it is simply considered an "alternate material," and granted a building permit only if an engineer can reasonably demonstrate that the materials will act as expected.

Thus was born the impetus to write this book: engineers have so far had little to work with in designing straw and earth structures. Even when open-minded or even enthusiastic, an engineer had to do a lot of reading, investigating, and research in order to develop the basis for a design and be able to rationally justify it to a building inspector.

Further complicating this effort has been the tendency towards unbridled enthusiasm and sweeping statements (usually innocent) among those who have been promoting alternate construction materials such as earth and straw. Elaborate or vague claims have been many; hard facts have been few. No one is to be criticized for this — a certain amount of drum-pounding and horn-tooting was perhaps necessary to get even the simplest projects built.

What was lacking in certifiable test results had to be made up with gut instinct, intuitive confidence, and enthusiasm. John Wesley Powell's description of one of his co-adventurers in the first descent of the Grand Canyon comes to mind: "He is a fine young man, skilled at hunting, trapping, and fighting, and he makes the most of it, for he is never encumbered by unnecessary scruples in giving to his narratives those embellishments that help to make a story complete."

The need for embellishment is now, happily, behind us. By carefully studying existing case histories and, where available, results of modern testing programs, we can now begin to define a rational basis for the structural design of earthen and straw-walled buildings.

Unfortunately, funding for research and testing, so urgently needed, has been scarce. With a few exceptions (which will be discussed), neither earth nor straw construction can be patented or turned into salable products, so industry has not seen much incentive to sponsor expensive structural tests. Nor has government at any level — also with some exceptions — been willing to underwrite the effort. The laws of economics will eventually change that as, for example, cement manufacturers realize that earth builders usually are consumers of their product, or as grain farmers, who can no longer burn their fields because of pollution controls, realize that straw-bale and straw-panel construction methods are outlets for their "waste" product.

Still, if these "alternate materials" are ever to gain legitimacy and move into the main body of the building codes and from the fringe of the construction industry to the mainstream, we need now to take a clear look at what we really know and what we still need to find out. The use of straw and earth in construction has been handsomely presented in *Build It with Bales, The Straw Bale House, The Rammed Earth House*, and other works (see bibliography). These are all thoughtful, useful studies which furnish essential information on their subjects. They are invaluable in providing an overview of the bigger picture and for the various details and considerations of doors, windows, fire safety, ventilation and moisture protection, etc., which will be treated only glancingly here. *Buildings of Earth and Straw* can be seen as a companion to those works, intended to fill in some of the technical gaps — specifically, to propose a means of structural understanding and analysis for earthen and straw-walled structures.

WHO WOULD WANT TO READ THIS BOOK, AND WHY?

Having set out to look carefully at these two "new" structural materials, I find I must address myself to two distinct audiences.

First is the owner-builder who wants to build his/her own earthen or straw-bale home (or office or daycare center or brew pub or other building). In my career as a structural engineering consultant, I have consistently found that people in the process of building — owners, carpenters, masons, etc. — are always interested in learning why things are done in some particular way: why the nailing is crucial here and not there, why the rebar should be placed just so, why and how the roof must be attached and vented, etc. They (you) may or may not want to learn very much about structural engineering. But you will very likely be told by your local building inspector to have an engineer prepare and stamp the plans. You will take your ideas and sketches to an engineer in your town — and then starts the mutual education.

That is why there is a second audience for this book, that very engineer, who must figure out how to help you design and build your project. Though I have tried throughout to present everything in the plainest possible terms and to make the basics of structural design comprehensible, I have also included what data, design technique, and analysis mathematics I could that an engineer needs to work with earth and straw as structures. In presenting the technical stuff I may, sooner or later, lose some of you in the first group of people. Alas, there's only so much I can do to demystify the 10-plus years of training and experience that your engineer went through to get licensed. It's not so easy to become, or be, an engineer.

> *One day during the French Revolution, a priest, a lawyer, and an engineer were convicted of being tools of the aristocracy and led to the guillotine. Declaring his faith in God, the priest refused a hood and insisted on being placed face up so he could see his fate. When the rope was cut, the blade would not fall! Everyone agreed it was a miracle and the priest was spared. The lawyer, having watched this, declared that he, too, would stand on his faith and meet the blade face on. Again, the blade didn't drop! And again it was declared a miracle, and the lawyer was set free.*
>
> *The engineer came forward and he, too, declared his faith and lay facing upward to be able to see the deadly blade. Again, the guillotine wouldn't fall! As the crowd again roared his vindication, the engineer squinted, peering up at the pulleys beside the blade, and slowly exclaimed, "Hey, I think I see the problem!"*

This joke, by the way, tells you Group One folks something a little bit useful that you might not have otherwise suspected about the Group Two folks. Notwithstanding a steady barrage of abusive humor about colorful personalities, or lack thereof, engineers in general are people who are intrigued by a good problem. And, being in a service business, we are (or should be) primarily concerned with helping a client get what he wants. So you who would build with alternate materials can, and should, regard your engineer as your friendly assistant. Convey your enthusiasm — make her/him part of your team. Present your ideas, make your points, ask all the questions you want, listen to what comes back, argue if you wish, but make the whole process informed, respectful, interactive, and open. (This sage and obvious advice applies equally — and perhaps even more — to your relationship with building inspectors.)

It will come as stunning news to many people in construction that your relationship with an engineer or building inspector need not be adversarial and can even be, well, friendly! Conversely, I have seen both the fun and profit quickly disappear from projects where open, respectful attitudes were not maintained all around. Forgive this tirade about the obvious, but, hey, it might save you some trouble and some money.

My intention, anyway, is that this book ease and facilitate the process of building with earth or straw (even if you Group One folks are left partially mystified by the engineering, and you Group Two engineers are left still a bit skeptical because there remains so much to be tested and learned). This book is a starting point, a statement of what we now know, which I fully trust will be expanded and improved upon in the years to come by myself and others.

EARTH AND STRAW: NATURAL COMPANIONS

Earth and straw: treated together here not just because they are "alternative materials," (i.e., not wood, steel, masonry, or concrete), but because they almost always have appeared together in the wonderful vernacular architectures of every continent. Our ancestors lived their lives in buildings of earth and straw, some of which were, yes, mere mud huts and grass shacks, while many were beautiful, intelligent structures far better suited to their climates than much of today's manufactured housing.

Nevertheless, straw and earth are two separate things: the many differences between, say, a rammed earth wall and a plastered straw-bale wall are important to recognize. Structure, cost, labor input, appearance, and, perhaps most importantly, thermal performance are radically different from one wall system to the next. Merely because earth and straw walls are not wood stud walls or concrete or masonry walls, many people have tended to regard them as equivalent. They emphatically are not, and you as the designer and/or builder of a structure must clearly evaluate the options in light of the many needs, assets, and limitations of your project.

Stabilized (and unstabilized) earth buildings can be found on every continent, some having been occupied for dozens, hundreds, or even thousands of years. A large part of the world's population still lives in earthen homes today. We therefore know that earth-walled buildings can be made and maintained to last and to provide safe shelter. Likewise there are hundreds, perhaps thousands, of years of history of straw construction throughout the world, and load-bearing straw-bale houses have survived for more than 90 years (and counting) in western Nebraska.

It is also true that many earth and straw buildings do not last very long, due to limitations of knowledge, resources, or both. Contemporary newspapers periodically report earthquakes in undeveloped parts of the world that cause multiple deaths due to collapse of masonry, earth, or concrete buildings. Even without earthquakes, wind, ice, and rain alone can fairly quickly return an improperly built earth or straw structure to the ground. It can even get a bit comical; grass and plants will sometimes sprout from earth walls and cattle will, given the chance, eat a straw-bale wall. Many builders are out there experimenting, so there were and are, inevitably, some failures. Or, perhaps we should say, unusual successes.

Buildings of Earth and Straw hopes to educate, inform, and make easier the design and construction of your earth or straw building. There are already straw-bale office buildings, rammed earth apartments, gun-earth wineries, and houses, houses, houses of every possible combination of these and other materials. Or, rather, every combination that's been conceived so far — many more are sure to come. What do you have in mind? Whatever it may be, this book hopes to provide some useful help and give your ideas a firm foundation.

WHAT WE WILL AND WILL NOT TALK ABOUT

Before we go too far, it seems only fair to spell out exactly what this book covers and what it ignores. *Buildings of Earth and Straw* looks at how earth and straw structures behave, what special construction requirements they present, and how to define, analyze, and specify earth and straw as structural materials.

Under the category "earth," or stabilized earth, are:

- *rammed earth* — a mix of soil, sand, water, and (usually) some other ingredient as stabilizer, which is mechanically compacted into forms that are then stripped off, allowing the mix to cure.

- *gunearth* (gunned earth) — similar earth mixes applied pneumatically through hoses using adapted gunite technology. (In his years of pioneering work in California, David Easton has adopted the term "pisé" for gunearth, both as an acronym for "pneumatically impacted stabilized earth" and in reference to the traditional French term for rammed earth (*pisé de terre*). The term pisé has become somewhat synonymous with gunearth around the West, but as it is, in this sense, proprietary, we will continue from here on using the term "gunearth.")

This leaves a number of other earth construction methods, some of which are well covered by existing literature (see bibliography), others of which should probably someday receive more attention:

- *adobe* — unfired bricks of clay, sand, and straw, usually laid like bricks in mud (adobe) mortar. Under this category could also be included poured adobe — walls of adobe slurry poured into forms.

- *compressed block* — similar to adobe, only rammed into the molds for greater density, strength, and durability. Commercial versions, under various trade names, are being made and sold in the USA and Europe.

- *cob* and *wattle-and-daub* — wall construction that in one way or another involves laying and packing dense clots of mud, often with a reinforcing framework of sticks (wattle) or straw reinforcing. Along with adobe, this is one of the most common forms of residential construction in the world.

- *ceramic architecture* — vaulted and domed structures of adobe block, fired, as kilns are, to vitrify the adobe. This method is being pioneered in Hesperia, California, by architect Nader Khalili.

- *tire houses* — structures formed by stacking used automobile and truck tires into walls, packing the centers with stabilized or adobe earth. This method was pioneered in Taos, New Mexico, by Michael Reynolds as a principal component of autonomous "Earthships" and has been developed more conventionally by residential builder Ed Paschich in Corralles, New Mexico.

- *concrete, concrete block, stone masonry,* and *fired-clay masonry* — in other words, the cement, rocks, and bricks with which we are all familiar. Stupendous volumes of testing, experimenting, research, and field study already have been published on these methods. It is worth noting, however, that these are also, in a slightly broader sense, stabilized earth construction.

For that matter, if you broaden the definition just slightly, the cellulose building materials — wood and straw — are earth stabilized with water, solar energy, and transformative biological mechanisms. And then, feeling giddy with philosophical insight, you see that not only are all building materials, even the most toxic petrochemical products, earth raised up and rearranged, but that pretty much everything you've ever touched, walked on, or eaten came from the same rocks and dust, including, yes, you. And all of that came, according to astronomers, from the expelled innards of expired stars; it's all stardust, it's all solar energy. So here, right at the start of this little book, you've had the true nature of the world explained for you, purely as a bonus. (Everything, that is, except what consciousness is. That you just have to look into for yourself.) What all this has to do with you building your house, I don't know. Maybe nothing, maybe something. But my digression is short and sweet; from here on out, stabilized earth will simply refer to rammed earth or gunearth.

The use of straw as a structural building material falls within the broader category of plant-based, fibrous, or cellular building materials; straw is the cousin of wood. Though usually thought of as the unused product of farm grains such as wheat or rice, straw from wild grasses, bamboos, sugar cane, corn husks, hemp, and other fibers has been or can be turned into useful building components. Two particular types of straw-based construction materials merit study:

- *straw bales* — compressed blocks of straw bound with steel wire or polypropylene twine and stacked like masonry.
- *straw panels* — manufactured panels of compressed straw in a wide range of densities, strengths, finishes, and other qualities.

Other (non-structural) straw construction methods include:

- *thatch* — laying straw or fibrous leaves as a roofing material — a highly developed art in the British Isles, Japan, Polynesia, Africa, South America, and elsewhere.
- *insulation* — using loose or bundled straw to fill cavities and holes in any other type of roof or wall system.
- *straw panel* — same as above, only lower-grade panels used just for facing, temporary formwork, paneling, etc.
- *leicht lehm* — light clay; infill made from coating loose straw with a clay slurry, which is then placed into forms or between studs in a wood-framed building. When the slurry dries, the straw holds its shape and has some insulating but no structural value. This is a very old technique from Europe.

There exists, then, a spectrum of structural building methods involving varying combinations of earth and straw. On one extreme are buildings made principally of straw — straw panel and straw-bale structures. On the other extreme are the pure stabilized earth structures of rammed earth or gunearth. In-between are the structural and semi-structural methods utilizing both earth and straw in varying ways — adobe, compressed block, cob, and leicht lehm. Although many of these methods have long track records, the wide array of possible permutations has yet to be fully explored. As time goes by, architects and builders will no doubt continue to experiment and develop (or relearn) the optimal system or combination of systems for particular sites and regions. These other materials and systems are, however, beyond the scope of this book.

A FOOTNOTE ABOUT BAMBOO . . .

In the course of looking at rammed earth and straw-bale construction, the use of bamboo continually comes up, for it is oftentimes used instead of steel for stabilized earth (and concrete) reinforcing, and for straw-bale pinning. After only a very cursory look into the structural uses of bamboo, a number of noteworthy points came up that bear passing along to the readers of this book.

There are over 1,500 varieties of bamboo growing between latitudes 50 degrees north and south of the equator and from sea level to timberline. For longer than recorded history, human beings have used bamboo for shelter, tools, music, clothing, and food — it is arguably the most utilitarian plant in our world. Using bamboo as structure generally requires either a willingness to rebuild regularly (for it biodegrades like any other cellular material) or a knowledgeable care in its harvest, cure, preparation, and installation in buildings. It has excellent tensile, compressive, and shear strengths and the bamboo plant itself (a "woody grass," in botanists' parlance) helped inspire the steel "tube frame" system used to stabilize many modern high-rise buildings. Bamboo is currently used as concrete reinforcing in areas where steel rebar is less available and was used experimentally in some structures at Clemson University in South Carolina several decades ago.

Bamboo fibers are also being used and studied as components of fiber-reinforced concrete, and bamboo fibers are being compressed into sheathing panels. The structural properties of the bigger, building-grade species have been well studied by engineers all over the world; sophisticated connections have been worked out; and magnificent new bamboo architecture is now emerging alongside the handsome traditional forms of native cultures throughout the world. It is only a matter of time before bamboo is "discovered" in the U.S. and other "developed" countries.

As a structural engineer, I am fascinated by bamboo and inclined to think that it makes a more-than-adequate low-grade reinforcing for concrete or stabilized earth (but not for use in high-occupancy or high-seismic-risk projects) and also works perfectly well for pinning straw bales. Having not yet made any sort of exhaustive study, however, I can only make these very superficial comments germane to earth and straw construction. Until someone makes a comprehensive presentation about architectural/structural bamboo to a North American audience, it is likely to remain largely unknown to our community of designers and builders.

And it's probably best left unknown, at least for now, for bamboo forests worldwide are already suffering from a surge in demand coupled with the spread of mechanized mass-harvesting techniques. Groves that had been sustainably harvested over many generations are now being overharvested or even clear-cut, and many consider the worldwide stock of key species to be endangered. Bamboo crops are already planted in limited patches around the United States, but far more would need to be planted and allowed time to mature before any appreciable demand can be met by domestic supplies.

A mature grove of bamboo can produce an extraordinary yearly harvest of buildable canes, effectively outproducing comparable forest building crops such as conifers. This fact will not go forever unnoticed, and I hope the next few years will see large-scale plantings of architectural bamboos in anticipation of increased demand in both the U.S. and the world at large.

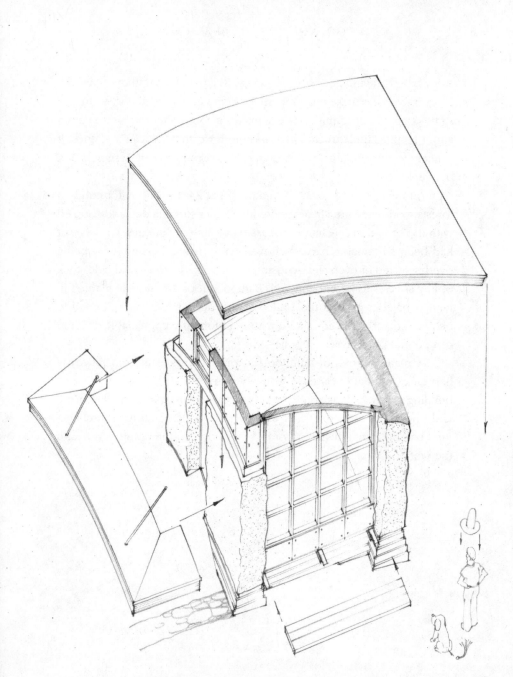

Real Goods Solar Living Center photovoltaic room
Courtesy of David Arkin, Arkin-Tilt Architects

part one

BASICS

"Come in," she said. *"I'll give you shelter from the storm."*

– Bob Dylan,
Shelter from the Storm

Carefully hidden elsewhere in this book are some of the formulas, graphs, and information that any professional engineer could use to design with earth or straw. And if you're at all in doubt as to how your building will A) get built, and B) survive all the destructive forces it will know in its lifetime, you should take your project to an engineer to work out the building system with you. You'll spend a little money, but you'll sleep better at night. *And* you'll probably have introduced another design professional to more ecologically sound ways of building. Someone did it for me, and it has been a delight.

Whether or not you do hire an engineer, though, you may — for a variety of reasons — want to be able to conceive of and design your building in the very precise language used to describe and analyze structures. With that in mind, this part has been written to familiarize you with the essential abbreviations, words, and concepts used in that specialized language.

As you study these terms, you may notice that they sometimes do and sometimes do not correspond to the same words as they are used and misused in common language. When you have learned the basic words of the trade, you will be able to impress your friends and building inspector, put your spouse to sleep, and get through the rest of this book with a minimum of confusion.

These terms (defined in a loose and simplified way, by engineering standards) will enable you, with or without the help of a design professional, to think about and design your own home (or workshop or office or pizza parlor or whatever).

The remainder of Part One is divided into the following three sections:

- Abbreviations and acronyms — common engineers' shorthand, spelled out
- Glossary — definitions of essential words and phrases
- Structures and forces — descriptions of building behavior and basic engineering concepts

ABBREVIATIONS AND ACRONYMS

ACI American Concrete Institute

AASHTO American Association of State Highway Transportation Officials

ASTM American Society for Testing and Materials

ICBO International Conference of Building Officials (authors of the UBC)

lbs pounds

OSB oriented strand board (panels of compressed wood chips)

PCA Portland Cement Association

pcf pounds per cubic foot

plf pounds per linear foot

psf pounds per square foot

psi pounds per square inch

UBC Uniform Building Code — see Glossary

UCBC Uniform Code for Building Conservation

GLOSSARY

*I know you believe you understand what you think I said, but
I'm not sure you realize that what you heard is not what I meant.*

— Richard Nixon

bending Pretty much as you've always thought of it; it would help to skip ahead to *moment* and *stress*. A moment acting on a body will induce bending stress, and will, well, bend it.

bond The measure of adhesion; the amount of stuck-togetherness of two objects. The bond of concrete or stabilized earth to reinforcing bars and anchor bolts is pretty important stuff.

bond beam A structural element within a wall (usually at the top) intended to stabilize the wall and facilitate the transfer of loads from above. The top plates in a stud wall could be thought of as a bond beam, though in this book it will generally refer to a wood or concrete assembly along the top of a straw-bale or stabilized earth wall.

buckling The collapse of a wall or column by bending and breaking under vertical load. The greater the unbraced length — the distance between bracing elements such as floors — the less load you can put on a wall before it will buckle. Take a yardstick, or any long, thin stick. Push down from above against the floor, and see how it bows out of shape — "column buckling," in engineering parlance. Now take the same stick, grasp it close to the floor, and push down; it can support far more force because the vertical (buckling) span has been reduced. If, for example, a 4x4 post that runs nine feet from floor to floor can carry about 6,000 lbs, then that same post, braced by a stair landing at midheight, can carry about 13,000 lbs. The mathematics are pretty involved, and beyond the scope of this book. Still, you'll need to know the concept.

cantilever Can be a noun or a verb, but either way refers to any structure or object that is rigidly secured at one end and completely unsecured at the other. Almost all trees cantilever up from the ground. You, standing in the wind, are a cantilever structure, as are diving boards, fishing poles, airplane wings — and your rammed earth or straw-bale wall, unless and until you brace the top.

compression forces (also see *stress*) Forces that tend to squish things together. Lie on the floor and have everyone at the party come sit on your back: compression! The opposite of *tension*. Bricks, concrete, and stabilized earth are all strong in compression and comparatively very weak in tension.

creep The slow deformation of an object or structure under load (if only its own selfweight). Bridges, bellies, and bales all sag with time; the rate of creep tells us how fast a given material loses its youthful vigor. Creep deformations are usually inelastic, i.e., they don't bounce back upon removal of load (contrast with definition of *modulus of elasticity*). *Creep* is also used to describe the ultra-slow-motion slide of a soil layer down a slope.

deflection A change of shape or position, such as the sag in a beam, movement at the top of a wall in an earthquake, or squashing of a loaded straw bale. A deflection can be temporary (elastic), permanent (inelastic), or some combination of the two.

diaphragm A plate structure: wide, flat, thin. Usually horizontal or sloped, such as plywood floors and roofs or concrete slabs. Diaphragms distribute forces among connected elements (such as a floor diaphragm distributing earthquake forces to supporting *shear walls*) and also braces them. (See illustration for *load path*.)

ductility The opposite of brittleness; used to describe a material's ability to yield by deforming, rather than suddenly breaking, and to absorb energy as it does so. Potato chips and cement plaster are brittle; cookie dough and straw bales are ductile, though just about everything becomes more brittle (less ductile) as it cools to or drops below freezing temperatures.

force An action that tends to cause a change of motion in a body. Isaac Newton said (and it's apparently still true) that bodies, or objects, in this world tend to keep doing whatever they're doing unless and until acted upon by an external force. This applies to baseballs, to a planet, to your feet, to government, and to a straw bale. To everything. Yes, this one is worth pondering. Newton sure did.

gunite A dry mix of sand, aggregate, and cement blown at high pressure through a hose, mixed in midair with a stream of pressurized water emerging from a parallel hose. This is a very loud and effective way to place concrete against formwork.

header The beam over a door or window that carries whatever *loads* are above.

in-plane shear (first read about *shear*) In-plane shear (or *force*) is shear parallel to the face of a wall — a load that tends to distort a rectangular wall into a parallelogram.

lintel A *header* over a window; a term usually associated with masonry construction, but also with earth and straw walls.

load Same as *force* — engineers categorize loads as follows: *dead loads (DL)* are the weight of anything permanent, chiefly the weight of the building itself or permanent elements of the building; *live loads (LL)* are any transitory forces such as snow, people, or temporary stacks of construction materials; and *lateral loads* are a category of live loads that are horizontal — mainly from wind, earth pressure (on retaining walls), and earthquake.

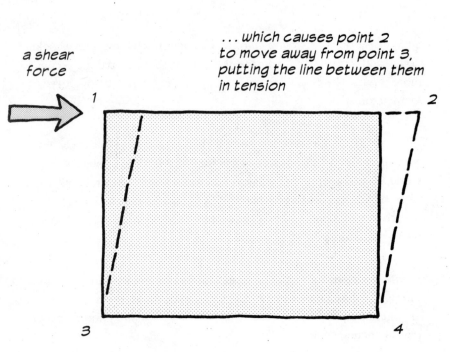

FIGURE 1. *a wall under in-plane shear*

load path Forces on buildings can be thought of like water or electrical current — they eventually will find their way to the ground. How they do that is via the load path, i.e., the route they find through the building structure. When the wind blows against your roof, your house doesn't start slithering across the ground like a snail, because Newton was right: for every action there is an equal and opposite reaction. The ground pushes back, exactly as hard. How the pushing "travels" from the surface of the roof to where your foundation meets the ground is the load path. And believe me, brothers and sisters, if you don't want your windows to crack or your doors to jam or your walls to wander, you'd better know your load paths.

modulus of elasticity (E) The measure of a material's stiffness, or springiness, or tendency to distort under load; the higher the value of E, the stiffer the material. Mathematically, it is the ratio of *stress* to *strain*. All you purists take note: this modulus only applies in the elastic range,

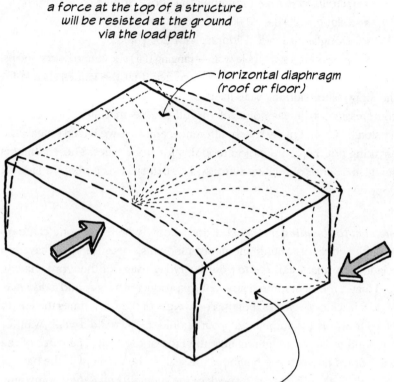

a force at the top of a structure
will be resisted at the ground
via the load path

horizontal diaphragm
(roof or floor)

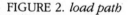

vertical diaphragms (shear walls)

FIGURE 2. *load path*

i.e., only under as much distortion as the material can take and still spring back to its original shape on removal of load. (Stand in front of the biggest window in your home at night, and lightly lob a tennis ball at it, noticing the distortion in the reflections; this was an elastic deflection, because the window regained its original shape. Now throw a heavy brick at the window; notice the inelastic deflection.) Understand this term; it is key in understanding how earth or straw behave when combined with plaster, wood, steel, etc. Here, for the sake of comparison, are the elastic moduli of some common materials:

- structural steel — 29,000,000 psi
- regular strength (2,500 psi) concrete — 2,850,000 psi

- stabilized earth — ranging (far) above and below 750,000 psi
- adobe walls — 80,000 to 120,000 psi
- Douglas fir grade 1 lumber — 1,700 psi
- unplastered straw-bale wall — ranging (far) above and below 150 psi

(It should be noted here, for accuracy, that the values shown for the straw-bale wall and stabilized earth are the moduli of elasticity in compression, whereas some of the others are moduli of elasticity in tension. It doesn't make much difference; anyway, we haven't measured anything but the compression modulus for straw bales. These numbers still give a sense of relative stiffness, i.e., that straw is perhaps a little bit floppy.)

moment (or bending moment) I don't know where someone came up with the idea of calling moments moments, because they have no relationship that I can see to your everyday usage of the word. Having said that: a moment is the mathematical product of a force and a distance. Hold a brick out at arm's length. The weight of the brick times the length of your arm is the moment at your shoulder. Or: build a wall. Wait for the wind to blow straight against the face of the wall. The *force* of the wind times one-half the height of the wall is the moment at the base of the wall. We sometimes also speak of the *moment capacity* of something like a beam, wall, or lintel — its ability to resist a moment.

moment of inertia (I) The stiffness of any object is a function not only of its constituent material's *modulus of elasticity*, but also the shape of the object's cross section; a 4x12 is less bouncy than a 6x8. Engineers have different ways of describing the same cross section, each for a different purpose, each based on elegant geometry that was worked out long ago. The cross-sectional area is used to calculate shear stresses, the *section modulus* is used to calculate bending stresses, and the *moment of inertia* is used to calculate deflections. The moment of inertia of a rectangular cross section is the width times the cube of the depth divided by 12 ($I = bh^3/12$).

out-of-plane load Out-of-plane load (or *pressure* or *shear*) is a *force* perpendicular to the face of a wall — a load that tends to push the face of the wall inward or pull it outward.

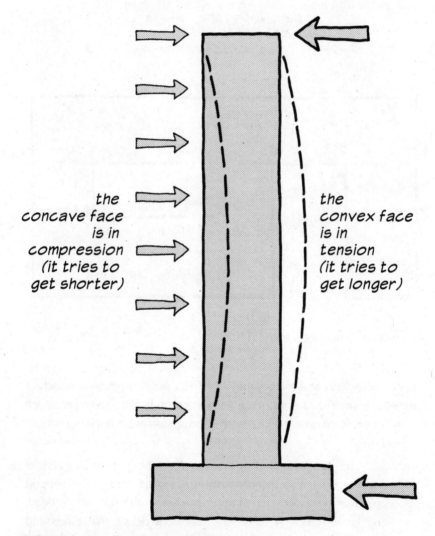

wind, earthquake, or liquid (earth) pressure
will bend the wall

the
concave face
is in
compression
(it tries to
get shorter)

the
convex face
is in
tension
(it tries to
get longer)

FIGURE 3. *a wall under out-of-plane loading*

pier Can be a number of things, such as a concrete-filled hole in the ground or a precast post for foundation support. In this book, however, pier will usually mean an element of a wall or a portion of a wall, e.g., the area between a door and the adjacent corner of the building. In designing walls of earth or straw, we have to look at piers within the walls, which are where *stresses* tend to concentrate and cause trouble.

*piers within the wall are
defined by ends and openings –
1-2-7-8, 3-4-9-10, and 5-6-11-12*

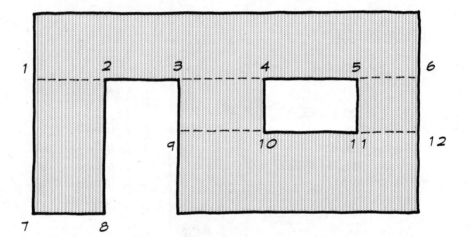

FIGURE 4. *a wall with piers*

pressure A *load* or *force* per unit area (e.g., pounds per square inch or tons per square foot). Pressure is always perpendicular to a surface, such as wind pressure on a wall or earth pressure against a retaining wall.

reaction The *force* provided by a support. If a body is holding still, as we generally want it to in construction, then the sum of the support reactions must be exactly equal and opposite to the sum of the dead, live, and lateral *loads*. A bathroom scale is a device that offers and broadcasts a vertical reaction — it tells you exactly how much upward force it takes to hold you up.

section modulus (S) The mathematical property of a cross section used to calculate bending stresses. The section modulus of a rectangular cross section is the width times the square of the depth divided by six ($bh^2/6$).

shear Can be a *force* or a *stress*, but either way a very specific beast — and an often-misused term. When two bodies are in contact, shear is any force acting between them parallel to the contact surface (90 degrees different from *pressure*). Put a brick on the table. Now push against the end of the brick so that it slides. The force you applied is a shear force, say, in pounds, and the shear stress is that same force divided by the

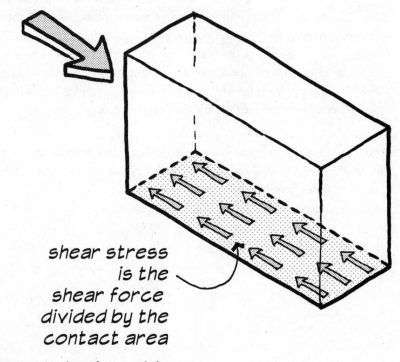

a shear force

shear stress
is the
shear force
divided by the
contact area

FIGURE 5. *shear force and shear stress*

contact face area of the brick, in this instance in pounds per square inch. Wind blowing on a house creates a shear force of the roof on the walls, and of the walls on the foundation; the shear stresses are those same forces divided by the respective contact areas. That's the basic idea, though it can, and usually does, get more complicated than that in a real building.

shear transfer The capacity of a joint or common surface to transmit shear forces between two bodies. You might know the shear capacities of two materials, but not know the *shear transfer capacity* when you stick them together — for example, plaster and straw bales, or rammed earth on concrete. There's a simple way to understand both shear transfer and its importance: make a plank bridge of two 2x4s laid one on top of the other. Make them span six feet or so between some support blocks. Stand on them, and have someone measure the deflection. Now get off, lay the planks on the ground, nail them solidly together (a 10-penny nail every six inches), and place them again on the supports. Stand on them again, and measure the new deflection. Such a difference! The nails, by creating shear transfer, kept the boards from sliding relative to each other, and made them act together. There are all sorts of places in a building where, by creating shear transfer, you can make two objects or materials act together to be stronger than the sum of the parts.

shear wall A structural wall intended to stabilize the surrounding structure by carrying shear (horizontal) loads imposed on the structure by wind, earth pressure, or earthquake.

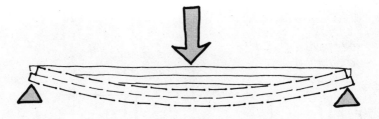

2 x 4 's free to slide will sag under load

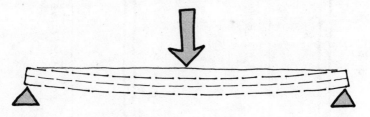

FIGURE 6. *2x4s with and without shear transfer*

strain Deflection or distortion per unit length, such as inches per inch (see also *modulus of elasticity*). A measured quality of a material distorting under *load,* key to understanding that material's stiffness. Very practical information for a bungee jumper to know about his cord, or for a straw-bale builder to know about her bales (e.g., "How much will this bungee cord stretch for each pound of tension I apply?" or, "How much will these bales squish when we get two feet of wet spring snow?").

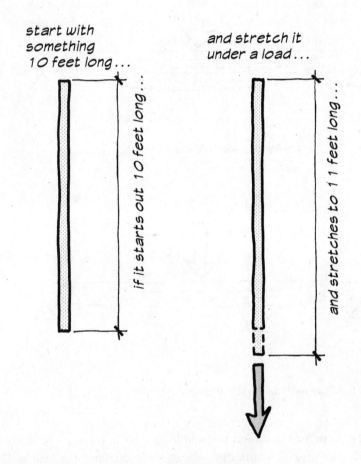

start with
something
10 feet long...

and stretch it
under a load...

if it starts out 10 feet long....

and stretches to 11 feet long....

...then the strain is 1/10, or 0.1 feet per foot
(this example is tension strain, but it works
the same way for compression, shear, etc.)

FIGURE 7. *strain*

stress Another often-misused term. In engineering, stress refers to the intensity of *force* within an object (force divided by area) that arises because of forces external to the object. You may have heard the joke about stress being the repressed desire to do extensive inelastic damage to your fellow human beings. These definitions are remarkably the same: *forces* in the environment of an object cause a state of stress, not necessarily visible, within the object. Dive to the bottom of a pool of water; the water around you is an external *force* (*pressure*), and the pain in your ears tells you, literally, about the resultant stress in your eardrums. In the example for *moment,* the muscular sensations in your back and shoulder are the *bending stress* that is the counterpoint of the external moment — the brick at the end of your arm. Stress comes in many flavors: bending, shear, compressive, tensile, bearing, torsion, temperature, shrinkage, etc. In a building or building element, just as in your skeleton or individual bones when you are active, several types of stress are usually present simultaneously.

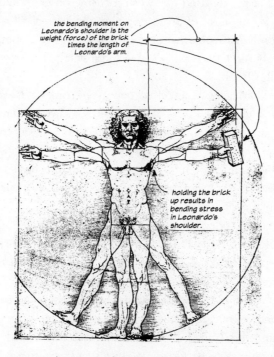

FIGURE 8. *moment/stress on shoulder (apologies to Leonardo da Vinci)*

tension   The opposite of compression, of course. Ropes and threaded rods and wires work great in tension, but are lousy in compression.

tributary area   Analagous to the watershed of a stream, the tributary area for a structural member such as a beam or wall is the total area of the building that must be supported, horizontally or vertically, by that member. If the distance between two bearing walls is 20 feet, then the tributary area for each is 10 feet wide.

Uniform Building Code (UBC)   The Bible, the Headache, the immoveable rock with slightly soft edges, and more. In the United States there are three main building codes, all fairly similar, each somewhat specialized to its domain: the Southern Building Code is used by the southern states and focuses on hurricanes, the Standard Building Code covers the East Coast and Midwest and attends to high wind and high snow loads, and the UBC is widely used out West, focusing on earthquakes. (As of this writing, a long-term effort to combine the best of all three into a single, comprehensive International Building Code is coming to imminent fruition.) The UBC is what I use, and it will be the reference code throughout this book.

Adopted into law by municipal, county, or sometimes state governments, your building code is the definer of safe building practice. Building departments and inspectors are charged with enforcing it, but are also given explicit authority to allow a project to deviate from it if a rational justification for doing so can be made. It also has some form of provision (section 104.2.8 in the UBC) for the use of "alternate materials" such as earth and straw.

Some see the code as an arbitrary and onerous burden on otherwise unfettered building projects (and, enforced in the wrong spirit, it can be), but keep in mind the positive: the building code is a tribal elder, the repository and distillation of much that we have learned about how and how not to build. It is an absolutely magnificent resource! Consider that in recent years earthquakes of about the same size have killed thousands in Azerbaijan, hundreds in Mexico, and exactly 59 in the crowded San Francisco Bay Area. The fact that there is currently almost nothing in the codes about earth or straw construction is a temporary omission that can be both an advantage and a disadvantage.

STRUCTURES AND FORCES

We live in a lively universe. Things are always changing, and nothing is ever quite as it appears to be. Take buildings, for example. There's no such thing as a static structure: somewhat like your body, your house is a dynamic organism with skin, respiratory, circulatory, nervous, and excretory systems; bones, eyes, feet, unmentionables, everything. Now that we've gone over some basic concepts and terms for structures, we can look at how a building behaves so as to inform your thinking about how to build, what to build with, and how to maintain your home.

Physical Forces That Act On Structures

On a molecular level, of course, all the constituent atoms and subatomic particles of all those deceptively calm items like linoleum and dirt and doorknobs are just swirling around like crazy. If quantum mechanics, however, was complex and inscrutable enough to confound such giants as Einstein, Bohr, and Heisenberg, then maybe it's best that you and I just amble on past that subject. The world of our everyday experience is swirling and crazy enough by itself, including the life of buildings.

Consider:

Whenever there is a change in temperature, things expand and contract, and different materials change at different rates. If it's 35 degrees on a sunny day, the shady side of the house is contracted, while the warm, sunny side is trying to expand — and they're connected, so something must give. If it's 10 degrees outside and 65 degrees inside, then there's lots happening in the walls and roof — a temperature gradient — which is stressing materials, and usually bringing out the mischievous qualities of water vapor in the air. Most things swell up

*temperature changes can bend and stress
any object, such as a wall or roof --*

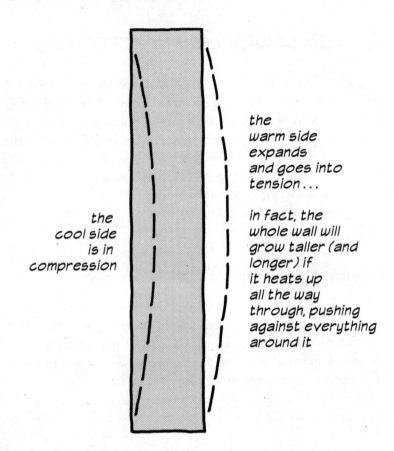

*the
warm side
expands
and goes into
tension...*

*in fact, the
whole wall will
grow taller (and
longer) if
it heats up
all the way
through, pushing
against everything
around it*

*the
cool side
is in
compression*

FIGURE 9.   *unevenly heated wall*

when they get wet and press hard against anything that tries to restrain them.

And there's the ground: sometimes it slides away or settles or, if you are on certain clay soils, expands when wet (which can and does shred improperly built buildings). Or sometimes the ground just washes out — in a single dramatic event or slowly, over time.

And there are the dead and live loads: a building must hold itself up and hold up any and all people and equipment that might come through — the car in the garage, the wild party/religious procession on the deck, the new hot tub in the bathroom, and the new roofing shingles that were all stacked in one corner over a window. Snow loads can be a category all in themselves; snow can be dry (light) or wet (heavy) and can accumulate or blow into deep drifts to particular areas of a roof (or next to a wall). Ice dams form on eaves where the melted snow (from the heat in the house) ran down to the (unheated surface of the) overhanging eave and refroze. That ice dam can get to be several feet thick and can literally crush an eave.

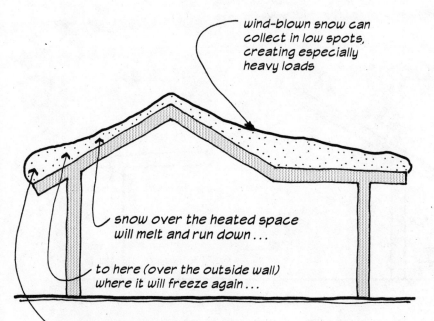

wind-blown snow can collect in low spots, creating especially heavy loads

snow over the heated space will melt and run down...

to here (over the outside wall) where it will freeze again...

creating a dam of heavy ice that will keep growing, and can break an eave

FIGURE 10. *snow loading*

And then you have to think about wind. A good hurricane can peel the entire roof off a house like the hat from your head. Even if you don't live in hurricane country, every couple of dozen years or so a pretty good gust is likely to blow on past, and it will find out for itself whether you built things right. (I was in Hurricane David in Florida in 1979; I weigh 200 pounds, and found it difficult — and frightening — to cross a small courtyard between two buildings.)

The wind will push on the windward face of your building, pull on the downwind side, and the eddying uplifts will push up on the overhanging eaves. It will literally suck shingles off the roof and can pick up a small rock, throw it through your window like a careless thief, then pop the rest of your windows from the inside. If you have any doubts

in a river, the current is not always moving
downstream - as the water flows around
rocks and corners, the current at any point
might be in any direction: upstream,
downstream, or sideways.

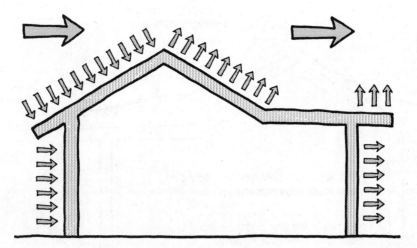

likewise, the wind pressures on a house
can and will be in any direction -
and can quickly reverse

FIGURE 11. *wind loading*

about the power of moving air, then think about what's holding you and your companions up next time you fly somewhere.

And then there are earthquakes! For structural engineers — and for you in a building — earthquakes belong in a category by themselves, for several reasons. First, they are (to date) unpredictable; the Big One can and does hit suddenly, with no warning at all. We now have the ability to see snowstorms and hurricanes coming, and have at least some time to prepare, but the Big Shaker just shows up like the worst sort of party crasher.

Second, earthquake forces are dynamic: they reverse, repeat, and come from any and all directions, including up and down; then, after ceasing, they repeat the process again a few minutes and/or hours and/or days later (aftershocks). Ride a fast bus on a busy, potholed, twisting

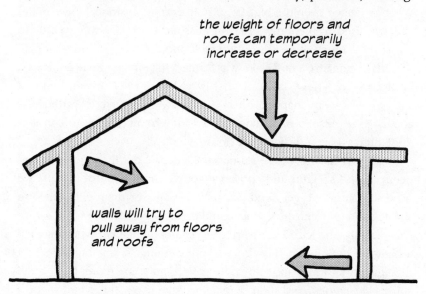

the weight of floors and
roofs can temporarily
increase or decrease

walls will try to
pull away from floors
and roofs

the foundation will jump
or slide or hammer out
from under the walls

any of the types of loads shown
can and will be in any direction -
and can instantly reverse

FIGURE 12. *seismic loading*

urban street for a few blocks, and you have a pretty good slow-motion earthquake simulation. As you do so, notice the difference between trying to balance on just your feet, and then holding onto a support at waist or shoulder level. This will inform your understanding when we talk about walls that cantilever from their foundations versus walls that are supported at the top by a floor or roof diaphragm: easier on the feet and legs, but that hand support had better be firm.

Finally, seismic forces can be really, really big. Although earthquakes happen by the thousands every day on the crust of our kinetic, crinkly little planet, the vast majority are too small to be felt; even most of those that can be felt generate less lateral force than a good strong wind. Still, in certain areas, at any time, the Big One can happen, generating tremendous destructive forces in every structure in the area. What may have been the biggest seismic event in historical times in the USA occurred in the early 1800s in Missouri (yes, Missouri, and there hasn't been much there since, but, well, there it was, and there it may someday be again); a huge lake was formed, the Mississippi River flowed backwards for a few days, and hardwood trees over several hundred square miles were snapped off at the trunk. If you live in earthquake country (see seismic zone map, page 156), you may want to consider these things as you design your house.

By now maybe you're starting to understand why structural engineers can be so grim and conservative: we think about this stuff. We obsess about it. We get hired not just to design a structure, but then to sit back and try to imagine what could possibly go wrong with it. A case was recently publicized of a very well regarded engineer who designed a high-rise building in New York City. Even after it was built, he kept thinking about it. He thought some more, and some more, and he did some calculations, and then, I imagine, stared out the window for a while. Then he picked up the phone, called his client, and said it won't work — a hurricane could bring it down — we need to fix it. And fix it they did. The happy ending: various parties managed to cover the expensive fix, and there were no lawsuits. After the story was made public, that engineer received letters from other engineers all over the country thanking him for his courage and describing similar situations they had privately experienced and dealt with. Astonishing as it may seem, engineering is an art as much as a science and, as with everything else in life, our knowledge is perhaps just slightly imperfect.

Engineering design — whether done (effectively) by you, or by a registered professional — depends not just on theory and numbers, but on creativity and common sense. Some of the more spectacular structural failures of our time resulted not from an arithmetic error deep in the fine print of labyrinthine calculations, but from a failure to imagine and comprehend the whole of the structure and how it would behave in nature. If you don't get the big picture right, the calculations don't mean much.

> *Structural engineering is the art of molding materials we do not wholly understand into shapes we cannot precisely analyze so as to withstand forces we cannot really assess, in such a way that the community at large has no reason to suspect the extent of our ignorance.*
>
> — William LeMessurier

If the project you are contemplating is small and simple — *hey, it's just a house, not a stadium* — then, yes, of course the design is made a lot easier. Even so, since you are (presumably) thinking of building with earth or straw, keep in mind that your hapless engineer may have only this meager volume to guide his or her thinking. We now have a reasonable body of knowledge with which to design, but are clearly still on the learning curve with these materials. An extra dose of caution is more than appropriate.

Some Other Variables

Besides God's own forces, there are three other factors that will affect your design: laws (codes), lawsuits, and budget. In the affluent, industrialized nations, building codes tend to be both sophisticated and enforced, generally in proportion to the local population density. I have had to devote weeks of my time, and thousands of dollars in engineering fees to my client, to draw and redraw plans for a simple, one-story, one-bedroom house in the San Francisco Bay Area, for no other reason

What you will have to consider as you design and build...

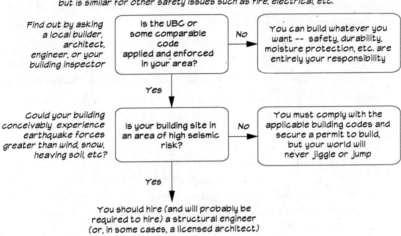

FIGURE 13.   *design criteria flowchart*

than to satisfy zealous, immature code enforcement. By contrast, I have designed substantially larger structures high in the storm-battered Rockies where the UBC was in force but there was no building department at all. In that case, I could work with my client to develop the structure to a reasonable level of safety without adding on extra structural costs of marginal value. If your property is in an area where codes are enforced, then you will, like it or not, be obliged to build into your structure a high margin of safety.

It should probably also be flatly mentioned that fear of litigation generally affects all parties involved in modern building design, at least in the U.S. Although you may not personally be so inclined, the viruslike propensity to capriciously litigate has fully infected our culture and is likely to affect your project, if only indirectly. Architects, engineers, builders, lenders, and insurers sometimes become conservative and gun-shy, unwilling to take even reasonable, modest risks. You will have to work with and around this pervasive attitude of fear, and artfully demonstrate why earth/straw construction is in fact a good idea. It is to be hoped that we as a culture will soon snap out of it and get on with life, accepting risks and responsibility rather than forever accusing and blaming. But for now, the lawsuits abound and the results influence all building projects.

In any case, within the constraints of the code, the design of your house will then be governed by your budget — a whole subject in itself. One small word of advice about that: don't kid yourself. Make a conservative estimate of all your costs at the start, and then add on some extra. It'll still probably cost more than that. That's just the way building projects usually go.

So. Now that you've established where you and your project stand with regard to codes, lawyers, and your available money, we can look briefly at what goes into any building structure. From there we will go on to explore earth (Part Two) and straw (Part Three) structures in more detail.

Foundations

The foundation must provide support for all loads, a stable base for the walls, and a moisture or capillary break between the ground and the building. (Although many historic buildings have been founded directly on the ground, or on gravel-filled trenches, and have lasted for decades or even centuries, others have been severely damaged by moisture wicking up the wall.) The support must also be stiff enough to prevent uneven settling, which can cause cracking.

Modern building codes, especially in seismic risk areas, generally require a stout, reinforced concrete foundation strong enough to span soft spots in the ground and firmly tied to the supported structure. If you're on a steep hillside, the foundation must allow for soil creeping down the slope from above, and hold the ground well enough not to slide. Good foundation design depends chiefly on understanding the site soil conditions, local climate, and appropriate foundation systems. You can usually find out from local builders, architects, engineers, or building inspectors what foundation systems are most appropriate in your area.

Gravity Loads

The weight of the roof and floors must be borne by some manner of vertical structure — usually either bearing walls or posts and beams. Beams are sized depending on the spans and the tributary loads, generally getting deeper in proportion to the square of the span. The bearing capacity of walls and posts is inversely proportional to the square of their unsupported length (vertical span), because most vertical elements will buckle before they will actually crush.

The intrinsic stability of earth and straw-bale walls comes from their relatively great thickness; more specifically, the crucial ratio of height (h) to thickness (t), usually described as "h/t," is comparatively large. Code and engineering limitations on both earth and straw construction are described in terms of limitations of h/t ratios, as well as limitations on the ratio of unbraced horizontal wall length (l) to thickness, "l/t." In other words, given a certain wall type (thickness), you don't want it to get too long or too high without adding more support.

Another class of structures of interest to earth and straw builders combines vertical and horizontal members into seamless wholes: arches, vaults, and domes. Beautiful to the eye, inherently stable (if designed properly), tricky to build right, these types of buildings make particular sense where there is nothing with which to build horizontal roofs (i.e., wood, bamboo, steel, etc.). The art of the dome was developed and perfected by the desert-dwelling Persians and Turks, and arches are still their trademark architectural motif. A few arches and vaults have been tried in both rammed earth and straw bales, so far with only limited success. Still, the form holds natural promise for future projects, even if the technical engineering and construction problems are yet unsolved.

Lateral Loads

Wind and earthquake loads (by which we mean, roughly, the wind forces produced by a once-in-100-year storm, and the seismic forces generated by the nearest and largest credible or historical earthquake) fall in the general category of lateral loads on structures. Common sense, as well as experience, tells us that even very high winds are rarely a

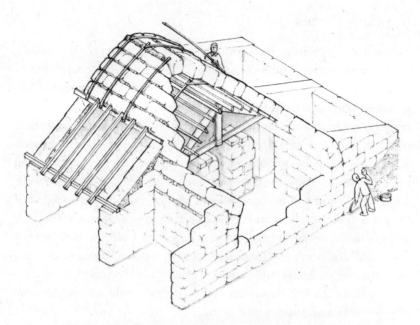

FIGURE 14. *straw-bale vault (Mongolia prototype), courtesy of Bob Theis, Dan Smith, and Kelly Lerner — Dan Smith and Associates Architects*

problem to stout straw-bale or earth-walled structures of one or two stories. (For higher buildings, such as the multistory earth-walled structures being built in western Australia, wind design becomes a major factor.) By contrast, earthquake forces will be larger in earth and plastered straw-bale walls than in wood-framed walls both because they are more massive — seismic force is in direct proportion to mass — and because they are more brittle. (Even in seismically active areas such as coastal California, wind loads on relatively light, wood-framed structures will often be higher than the forces generated by earthquakes.)

In designing structural walls, consideration must be given to in-plane forces and out-of-plane forces. During an earthquake or wind storm, both types of forces will be acting simultaneously in some combination. But it is common practice to analyze each separately, and then review the entire, three-dimensional structure for locations of stress concentration, connections, and coherence.

In-plane Forces

Any wall assembly intended to carry lateral forces of the building via in-plane shear is generally known as a shear wall. The amount of force that will go into the wall depends on the building geometry, the wall geometry (i.e., stiffness), and the stiffness of the floor or roof diaphragm carrying the loads into the wall. What are often called shear cracks in a wall are in fact tension cracks (see Figure 15), which develop when the wall racks and opposite corners move farther apart, creating a line of tension. Stabilized earth and the plaster skin on straw-bale walls are relatively weak in tension and will readily crack. If the direction of the loads reverses, as in an earthquake, matching diagonal cracks will open in the opposite direction. At this point, the fractured wall has lost some or all ability to resist tension or shear, and any subsequent shearing loads may be excessive and cause complete failure or collapse.

Portions of a wall beside openings — piers — will behave the same way — like miniature walls within the wall — and are likewise susceptible to tension cracking and failure. Openings in a wall will also

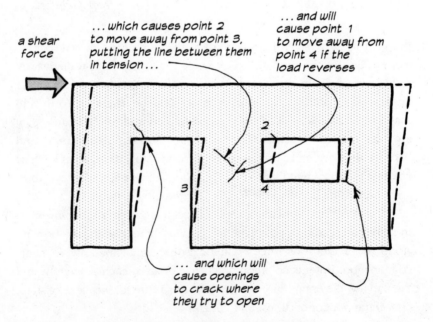

FIGURE 15. *a wall with piers under in-plane loading*

create stress (tension) concentrations as the wall tries to change shape under lateral loading. Thus, the size and location of openings (or, more exactly, piers) in a wall are crucial to the stability of the structure.

In designing a shear wall for in-plane forces, the following factors are important for assuring adequate strength, and can be adjusted in relation to each other:

- The strength of the finished wall assembly and its materials, including any reinforcing.
- The thickness of the (structural) wall — the wall's shear capacity increases with thickness, although the seismic loads from the wall's own weight, being directly in proportion to mass, also increase with increasing thickness.
- The presence (or lack) of redundancy or backup. Are there other walls nearby that can carry some of the load? Is there a good margin of safety? Is there a secondary system that could be engaged to hold things together if the primary system fails?

Out-of-plane Forces

How a wall will respond — bend — under load against its face will somewhat depend on how it is secured at the foundation and roof (or floors; see Figure 16). If the wall is restrained at the top, it can be considered to be pinned (free to rotate) top and bottom. Design of the top restraint for a structural wall in a seismically active area is both important and, assuming a wood-framed restraining floor or roof, somewhat difficult. The connection plates, bolts, and straps must be carefully designed and the floor or roof itself designed to be strong enough to act as a diaphragm capable of transmitting the reaction.

It bears repeating that for wind forces, the design of diaphragms and connections is not too difficult, particularly for residential structures of modest size and conventional shape. By contrast, in seismic risk areas, it becomes a very big deal and demands very careful attention. After the January 1994 earthquake in Northridge, California, engineers studied the various building failures. Germane to this book are the findings regarding tilt-up building failures. (*Tilt-up* refers to a type of construction, usually for warehouses, in which concrete walls are built flat on the ground and

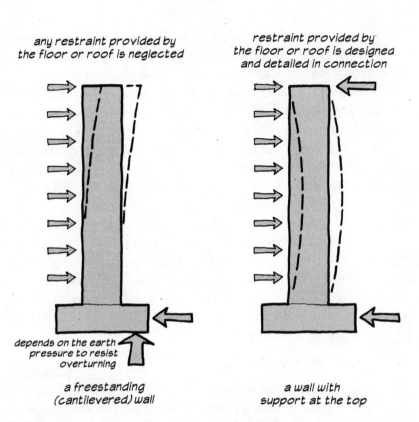

any restraint provided by
the floor or roof is neglected

restraint provided by
the floor or roof is designed
and detailed in connection

depends on the earth
pressure to resist
overturning

a freestanding
(cantilevered) wall

a wall with
support at the top

FIGURE 16. *cantilevered and top-supported walls*

then tilted up to their final, vertical positions. They then support, and
are braced by, wood-framed roofs, making them structurally similar to
both stabilized earth and plastered straw-bale buildings being erected
today.)

What they found in Northridge were connections between the roof
diaphragms and concrete walls that had completely failed, even though
designed and built according to modern code requirements; apparently,
the springy plywood diaphragms "hammered" the connected, rigid walls.
To summarize and simplify those findings, it was concluded that the
connection must be far stronger than the computed wall restraint alone
would need — if the wall requires, say, 500 pounds per linear foot of
restraint force to remain stable, then the connection to the bracing

diaphragm had best be designed for 750 or even 1,000 plf, and allow for some ductile yielding before failure.

An alternative is to consider that the wall is fixed at the foundation (cantilevered) and free (like a tree) at the top (even though attached structure will always provide some restraint, that restraint could then be considered redundant). In this system, the footing is made wide enough to give the wall stability against overturning. The supported roof or floor is then considered to "float" on the walls, which are self-supporting in an earthquake.

In either case, the absence or presence of crosswalls also comes into play. If corners and crosswalls are of the same construction (or something else of comparable strength and stiffness) and are properly tied to the supported wall, they then comprise vertical lines of support which can and should be considered in the design.

Earthquake Loads

Over the past few years, awareness has grown in the structural engineering community that the public at large, and our clients in particular, often misunderstand our contribution to building design. The biggest misconception is of invulnerability, and it cannot be overemphasized that there is no such thing as "earthquake-proof." The structural provisions in the Uniform Building Code are minimum standards intended to safeguard against major failures and loss of life, not to limit damage, maintain functions, or provide for easy repair. According to printed recommendations of the Seismology Committee of the Structural Engineers Association of California 1990 *Blue Book*, the following levels of performance are expected of structures designed according to current building codes and engineering practice:

"1. Resist a minor level of earthquake ground motion without damage.

"2. Resist a moderate level of earthquake ground motion without structural damage, but possibly experience some nonstructural damage.

"3. Resist a major level of earthquake ground motion having an intensity equal to the strongest either experienced or forecast for the building site, without collapse, but possibly with some structural as well as nonstructural damage."

For the purpose of calculation, earthquake forces are treated just like wind forces — maybe bigger, maybe smaller, but simply a horizontal force nonetheless. This type of thinking is common, but somewhat misleading. Even hurricane force winds, though tremendous, don't have the vibratory, impactful, erratic, or reversing qualities of an earthquake. Imagine a fine dining room table set with beautiful crystal glasses; the wind just tries to blow them off, but the earthquake is your drunken Uncle Barney who tries to yank the tablecloth from underneath them. Then he yanks a few more times, from different ends.

What this means to you, if your building is in a seismic risk area, is that you need more than just adequate strength in your walls; you need a large margin of safety and/or backup systems for carrying lateral forces, because you really can't predict that accurately the size of the forces that may happen (above and beyond the foregoing discussion regarding connections). For example, an earth wall in coastal California might be designed, per the UBC, for a lateral seismic load of 30 percent of its dead load. In a large earthquake, however, the forces might actually reach as high as 40, 50, or 80 percent of the dead load, in which case extra system capacity had better be there. Likewise, a straw-bale wall might have a cement plaster skin that theoretically can carry the calculated seismic loads, but, knowing how brittle stucco is, most designers also specify steel strapping or threaded rod braces as an additional system.

Of equal importance to the high safety margin is the design of ductility, or the capacity of the entire building to deform (absorb the energy of the earthquake) without collapsing. Car designers clearly understand this concept. I was once in an accident in which the car around me was thoroughly crushed and battered in such a way as to absorb all the energy of the impact, enabling me to unbuckle my seat belt and climb out unharmed. This was exactly what that car's designers had intended and successfully designed, and what a building designer must think about in seismically active areas.

Other Lateral Force Systems

In talking about earth and straw construction, we will inevitably be thinking about walls as primary structural elements. Keep in mind, however, that there is a large range of systems, and hybrid systems, for carrying both vertical and lateral loads. Roofs and floors can be supported by posts and beams, making the rest of the wall construction merely infill. Some designers surround earth walls with concrete frames — posts and beams — effectively taking all vertical and some lateral loads off of the (relatively weak) stabilized earth. And the New Mexico Building Code explicitly requires a post-and-beam system to surround straw-bale walls — load-bearing bales are disallowed (presumably because of the unknown elastic effects of cyclic, heavy snow loading, though this seems to me a premature and unscientific conclusion to have forged; load-bearing straw-bale construction may, with time, prove to be an impractical or unsafe system, but evidence to date strongly suggests otherwise).

There are also innumerable varieties of braced frames — relying on the simple fact that triangles of almost any sturdy material are stiff and strong — from a simple knee brace between a post and a supported beam to elaborate three-dimensional space frames designed to carry vertical and/or lateral loads over huge spans. There are also moment frames, whose strength depends not on triangulation but on rigid connection of the joints. (Most chairs are moment frames, relying for their stability on the stiffness of the joint between legs and seat.) And there are combinations of shear walls, braced frames, and moment frames; the possibilities are endless.

Many, if not most, earth and straw structures are simple rectangular buildings in which the walls are both bearing and shear walls. But many are not, and for one reason or another, posts, beams, braces, and/or rigid joints may become necessary elements of your project. The trick is to make everything work together — structurally, functionally, and aesthetically — to get the building you want.

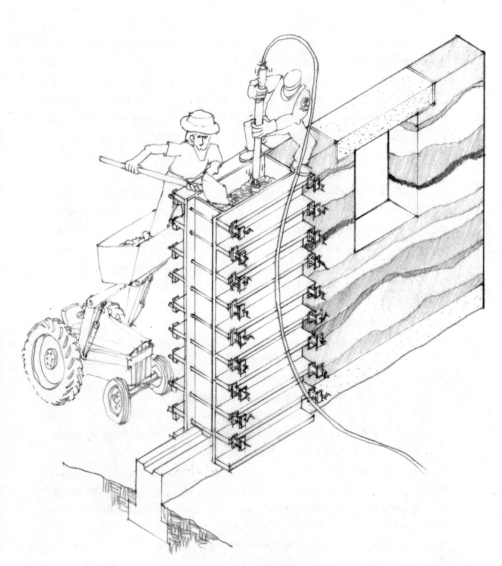

rammed earth wall
Courtesy of David Arkin, Arkin-Tilt Architects

part two

EARTH

*Father Latour had chosen for his study a room at one end of the wing.
It was a long room of an agreeable shape. The thick clay walls had
been finished on the inside by the deft palms of Indian women, and
had that irregular and intimate quality of things made entirely by the
human hand. There was a reassuring solidity and depth about those
walls, rounded at door-sills and window-sills, rounded at wide wings
about the corner fireplace. The interior had been newly whitewashed
in the Bishop's absence, and the flicker of the fire threw a rosy glow over
the wavy surfaces, never quite evenly flat, never a dead white, for the
ruddy color of the clay underneath gave a warm tone to the lime wash.*

— Willa Cather, *Death Comes for the Archbishop*

Earth construction is one of the earliest means of shelter that human beings ever created for themselves — some of the oldest buildings extant on Earth today are of earthen construction. Rammed earth buildings can be found on every continent, some having been occupied for hundreds or even thousands of years.

So we have a huge empirical basis for understanding and designing earth-walled buildings. With the recent adaptation of gunite technology for the construction of stabilized earth buildings, there are now two distinct categories (besides adobe and compressed adobe) of stabilized earth structures: rammed earth and pneumatically applied gunearth.

THE MATERIAL

We can start the discussion with a general look at stabilized earth — both the material and the building methods — and then look at distinctions between the categories of rammed earth and gunearth.

Stabilized Earth

In geology, there is a class of rock called conglomerate: a blend of sand and rock particles deposited together in some type of natural binder or cementitious matrix. This is exactly the model that stabilized earth emulates, for a stabilized earth wall is effectively an artificially constructed wall of rock. Rammed earth can emulate a particularly attractive type of conglomerate, or sedimentary rock, formed when successive layers of material of different colors are deposited one on top of another.

The constituent particles are themselves pieces of rock (organic soil, because it biodegrades, is unacceptable for stabilized earth construction and must be limited to 1 or 2 percent of the total mass, if allowed at all). They vary in size from the microscopic to, usually, not bigger than one inch (or however big a particle can be practically accommodated in the application). The sizes of particles are categorized by the size of screened mesh opening through which they can pass, and mixes of stabilized earth, like concrete, are defined by minimum and maximum percentages of material passing respective screens (see Appendix E-1). The ideal mix has a balanced proportion of large particles (gravel, from one inch to as small as about 3/16 inch), sand (from 3/16 inch to as small as a few thousandths of an inch), and fines — particles smaller than three-thousandths of an inch. The proportion of fines is of key concern in stabilized earth design, and there are two types, indistinguishable just with physical sieve tests. *Silt* is finely ground sand (smaller than three-thousandths of an inch), while *clay* is both smaller (less than one ten-thousandth of an inch) and different in its chemical reactions.

Clay particles are not the product of conventional erosion and grinding, but are formed from the leaching of rock and soil to produce hydrated alumino-silicates: long, platelike crystals with ionic charge. When wetted, they electrically attract each other (hence clay's plasticity when wet) and water (hence the swelling and then shrinkage cracks when clay soils become wet and then dry out).

The physical chemistry of clays is complex, and far beyond the scope of this work, but clearly the clay content in a stabilized earth mix must be controlled. Historic and durable earth-walled buildings derive their success from having achieved a good proportion of clays: enough to act as a binder, but not too much, and of the right type (minimum swell) so as not to stress or crack the finished wall. The suitability of a specific site's own soil for earth construction must be determined by test; initially, through field tests for clay and silt content, and then, if necessary, through lab tests for more specific knowledge of clay content (or expansion coefficient) and compressive strength. For an excellent and comprehensive review of the various soil tests, types, and the suitability of each for earth construction, refer to *The Rammed Earth House* by David Easton.

Thus, the final product, stabilized earth, is a rocklike blend of clay, silt, sand, gravel, water (some is always present in various forms), air (in microscopic bubbles and voids between the particles), and, usually, some binder. In many parts of the world earth construction is still practiced using only the clay content as binder. This approach is best suited, and perhaps best limited, to arid regions with minimal seismic activity (parts of Iran, western Australia, and New Mexico, for example). Where there is more moisture or earthquake activity, artificial binders should be used to ensure a higher level of cohesion in the material.

Some builders have experimented with lime, fly ash, asphalt emulsion, and combinations of these materials as soil binders. The strongest binder, however, is Portland cement, and this discussion will henceforth focus on stabilized earth, when artificially stabilized, using

sand and aggregate will ball up with clay
if the mixing is inadequate or wetted too soon,
resulting in soft lumps that weaken the
final stabilized earth wall

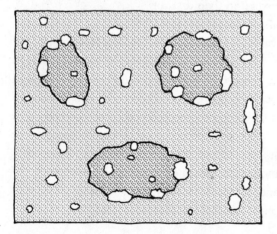

FIGURE 17. *clay balls*

cement as the principal binding agent. In such cases, thorough crushing and mixing of the dry materials is even more important, as is the need to control the clay content. Although clay and cement seem to act together to a limited extent as binders, they sometimes work at odds with each other. Excess clay tends to clump or ball up, effectively creating new lumps of low-strength aggregate that must be cemented.

Rammed Earth

As a material, rammed earth is similar to compressed adobe or unfired clay masonry. In physical composition it may be identical, but as a structural wall material it will always prove stronger because there are no mortar joints and the material is compacted in place (as were many of the first reinforced concrete structures). The finished material is nevertheless similar to masonry in that there are a series of semi-cold joints between lifts, and within each lift the density varies from highly compacted at or near the top (directly under the ramming head) to less densely packed below the top of the lift. (Both of these attributes will generally have little effect on the large-scale wall strength, unless lifts are thicker than five or six inches.)

Gunearth

Gunearth is lighter (because it contains more air) and more homogeneous than rammed earth and, all else being equal, is not as strong. It is uniform in appearance, not having the stratified rock appearance of rammed earth, but is far cheaper and faster to build. Gunearth, particularly in a thin veneer, will crack more than rammed earth, mainly because the higher water content causes more swelling of the clay in the mix.

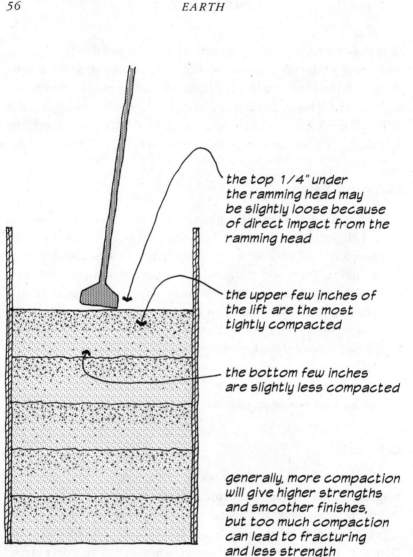

the top 1/4" under
the ramming head may
be slightly loose because
of direct impact from the
ramming head

the upper few inches of
the lift are the most
tightly compacted

the bottom few inches
are slightly less compacted

generally, more compaction
will give higher strengths
and smoother finishes,
but too much compaction
can lead to fracturing
and less strength

FIGURE 18. *rammed earth lifts*

Stabilized Earth Mix Design — A Case Study

The design of a mix to create a desired compressive strength (and, by inference, other types of strength) should be based on actual tests; theoretical prediction is not yet adequately reliable. The stabilizing addition of Portland cement to a soil blend makes what is called soil cement in the construction industry. Soil cement has been used extensively to date for paving, pond liners, and slope stabilization, and as such has been extensively studied as an engineering material. Much has been learned about the interaction and blending of the various soil types with cement, although that research has been focused on slope stabilization and highway subgrade construction, not load-bearing walls (see Appendix E-2).

For the present, the earth wall designer must generate a tentative design using accepted soil classification and investigation methods, then cure and test sample mixes for confirmation of desired properties. (Stabilized earth cures more slowly than concrete; the typical 28-day strength test used for concrete will generally only reveal about 60 or 70 percent of stabilized earth's long-term strength. If at all practical, a 56-day compression test will give a clearer picture for design.) Also, earth construction, like welding or applying gunite, requires a highly experienced crew to properly place the material. It cannot be overemphasized that quality control of on-site mixing, wetting, and compacting/gunning is essential to obtain design strength.

In the wine-growing region of Northern California (Napa, Sonoma, and Mendocino Counties), many dozens of earth-walled buildings have been erected over the past decades. When on-site or nearby soils have proven unsuitable for use in stabilized earth, most builders have used leftover fines (waste from gravel excavation and production) from the local Nun's Canyon Quarry. Nun's Canyon fines have a near-ideal blend of particle sizes (3/8-inch maximum) for achieving strength and a handsome orange-brown color that produces beautiful walls.

In the course of designing a very large stabilized earth house north of San Francisco, having established that local soils were unsuitable, we did an extensive amount of testing on stabilized earth blends using Nun's Canyon fines. The project included rammed earth, gunearth, and gunearth veneer, and the architecture did not always provide the wide roof overhang that is traditionally provided to shield stabilized earth from the worst of weather and moisture problems. We built test versions of rammed columns and gunned walls in the contractor's yard, also taking six-inch-diameter test cylinders. Besides giving us the chance to see color and texture, this also furnished the basic material for a wealth of subsequent tests. (When the job was just starting and this text was nearly completed, a new problem emerged in the project which should be mentioned, as it can easily happen to other stabilized earth projects. Nun's Canyon Quarry began excavating a different vein of material, and the soil we were offered was different, in both behavior and appearance, than that which we had tested. Fortunately, we were able to obtain enough of the old stock to meet our needs, but the lesson was clear: be certain of your material source at the outset of design.)

We developed a basic mix we came to know as "seven twenty-one" because of the mix proportions — seven parts Nun's Canyon fines to two parts sand to one part cement. Different color mixes were obtained with these same proportions by substituting white or tan cement for gray and/or adding colorizers. For rammed earth, water was added at about 13 percent of the dry mix weight. This amount yielded a mix of a consistency that, when balled up in the hand and dropped from waist height, broke into several coherent clods (neither shattering nor "splat-ting") — the universally recognized hand-drop test for moisturizing rammed earth. This corresponds to a water-to-cement ratio of about 63 percent — higher than with conventional concrete, and presumably more than enough to engage and hydrate all the cement if fully mixed. The gunearth mix had slightly more water.

We found that, as with concrete, the earth and sand must have the right pH levels so as not to interfere with the hydration of cement — excessive salts (i.e., high pH or high alkalinity) will impair strength and lead to extensive efflorescing. (Old foundations in California that used unwashed beach sand in the concrete are now so soft they can be scored with a key.)

An abridged summary of our testing results follows. Each value represents the average of at least three tests of the given type, but there was a large statistical scatter in most cases (just as will happen in compression testing of concrete cylinders). Also, the compressive strengths we saw were generally higher than we expected, probably due to the relatively high cement content and to the high degree of ramming we needed to get a very clean architectural finish.

■ density and chemistry tests

We established that Nun's Canyon fines are a type M145 A-2-4 soil in the AASHTO classification system (type D2487 soil in the ASTM system), has a liquid limit of 30, a plastic limit of 21, and a plasticity index of 9. The soil itself has a pH of about 4.0, but the cured stabilized earth (both rammed and gunned) had a pH of 10.5. (A sample of ordinary concrete had a pH of 11.2.) The cured density of rammed earth was 129 pcf; the cured gunearth was 117 pcf.

■ compressive strength tests

Using standard ASTM compression tests for cylinders and cores, we got the following results (in psi):

	@14 days	@35 days	@90 days	@126 days	@215 days
rammed	1420	2630		3395	3890
gunned	1710	1993	2087		

We generally found a surprisingly high two-week strength, a very wide scatter in the test results (especially for rammed material — up to 150 percent difference in a batch), and appreciable continued strength gain after seven or eight weeks.

■ moisture exposure tests

Because some gunearth walls would act as retaining walls, we wanted to explore the effects of potential moisture intrusions on strength (despite the inclusion of extensive moisture protection measures; unstabilized earthen structures that go through repeated wet-dry cycles lose strength). We took 12 three-inch-diameter cores from gunearth panels and tested four sets of three at 105 days old. The results were:

- Control (not wetted) had an average strength of 1,660 psi (the puzzling difference — 1,660 psi @ 105 days vs. 2,087 psi @ 90 days, as shown above — was never fully clear to us, although the values were derived from different batches shot and cured in different conditions).

- 14 days of constant immersion showed a 40 percent average loss of strength.

- 14 days of constant immersion in water halfway up the cylinder showed a 19 percent average loss of strength.

- 14 days of 16 hours/day total immersion and 8 hours/day of drying showed a 15 percent average loss of strength.

It should be observed, however, that subsequent longer-term tests, as well as old AASHTO tests on highway soil-cement subgrades, suggest that long-term loss of strength due to moisture exposure is less severe than these results imply, and may sometimes even *increase* strength.

■ bond strength tests

Pieces of #4 grade 40 reinforcing bar that had been encased in the gunearth panels were tension-tested to failure, with the following results:

bar	embedment (inches)	failure load (pounds)	bond stress (psi)	failure mode
1	4.5	6,100	863	cone failure
2	12	11,500	610	rebar yield
3	19	12,200	402	rebar yield

■ fastener tests

A two-foot cube of rammed earth was built and cured for four months to test various fasteners. Three or four tension and shear tests were done on each, using different orientations to the rammed lifts. Although some tests were only taken to manufacturer's proof load (not failure), average values are summarized below.

- $1/4$-inch diameter, 3.75-inch self-tapping masonry screws (Tap-con by Ramset/Redhead Corp.):
  - average shear load 800 pounds; failure mode — crushing of stabilized earth
  - average tension load 2,075 pounds; failure mode — cone failure of stabilized earth
- $5/8$-inch diameter epoxied bolts embedded 6 inches (CIA GEL-7000 by Covert Operations, Inc.):
  - average shear load 6,475 pounds; failure mode — crushing of stabilized earth
  - average tension load 11,313 pounds; failure mode — cone failure of stabilized eart
- $5/8$-inch diameter wedge bolts embedded $6\,5/8$ inches (Trubolt by Ramset/Redhead Corp.):
  - average shear load 5,700 pounds; failure mode — crushing of stabilized earth
  - average tension load 6,500 pounds; failure mode — slippage of anchor

■ admixture tests

In an effort to reduce permeability (to protect the interior, avoid possible strength degradation, and reduce efflorescence), we considered a number of concrete admixtures to try with stabilized earth. Many, such as silica fume, were immediately rejected because of excessive color effects (darkening). We ended up trying three options, each of which in one way or another decreases permeability in concrete by filling void spaces. We inferred that they might have the same effect on stabilized earth.

In all cases, strength decreased between 10 and 30 percent, with no clear decrease in permeability or efflorescence. However, we had no effective means of testing for permeability or efflorescence, nor the time to generate dependable results; further research might reveal promising benefits of any or all of these additives.

The three admixtures are described below.

- Liquid butyl stearate acid-based compound (Rheomix 235® by Master Builders, Inc.), which fills void spaces with an insoluble fatty acid, thereby retarding moisture penetration.
- Crystal-producing compound (Xypex® by Xypex Corp.), with a secret formula that includes Portland cement and fine silica sand, which reacts with water to grow crystalline fibers that penetrate and fill void spaces. We added at the recommended 3 pounds per 100 pounds of cement, but found that exceeding that dosage greatly retarded both set and strength.
- Fly ash, pozzolanic (semi-cementitious) waste product of coal-burning power plants whose use as a cement substitute is now common in modern construction. In the U.S., Class C fly ash comes from the relatively high-sulfur lignite coal of the Appalachian Mountains and becomes somewhat cementitious with the addition of water. The anthracite and bituminous coals of the western U.S. produce Class F fly ash, whose use in concrete is limited to 25 percent of the Portland cement volume because it relies on a chemical reaction with the Portland cement to become cementitious. Fly ash generally slows and cools the set of concrete in the short-term and decreases both permeability and efflorescence. We substituted Class F fly ash for 25 percent of the cement in the 7-2-1 mix (both rammed and gunned).

■ absorptivity tests

The "sponge effect" was measured by comparing weights of soaked vs. oven-dried samples. We found that plain concrete could absorb 7.2 percent of its weight in water, rammed earth could absorb 11.5 percent of its weight, and gunearth 15.8 percent.

■ erosion and wear resistance tests

The material loss effects of a high-pressure blast of water (erosion) and a rotating steel grinder (wear resistance) were measured. Compared to 50-day-old concrete, 35-day-old rammed earth was two times less resistant to erosion and four times less resistant to wear. Ninety-day-old gunearth was three times less resistant to erosion and 36 times less resistant to wear. The testing was by no means comprehensive enough to draw anything more than broad conclusions; I particularly suspect that the gunearth, though clearly softer than concrete, is really harder than the test results suggest.

ANALYSIS

An engineering analysis sees rammed earth and gunearth as very nearly the same, so this discussion addresses stabilized earth in general. Differences between the two materials are discussed later, under the heading "Design and Construction Considerations." In seismically active areas, earthquakes are by far the dominant consideration in earth wall analysis. Therefore, this discussion will start with design in non-seismic areas, where a cement binder and reinforcing bars may be optional. Design for seismically active areas follows.

Design in Non-seismic Areas

Material strength varies widely with the quality of the mix design. Some earth mixes can attain compressive strengths better than 900 psi without added binder, while others can barely manage 300 psi even with two sacks of cement per cubic yard added (usually because of too high a proportion of silt fines "soaking up" or, in a sense, diluting the available binder). Generally, increasing the amount of binder increases strength. Further variables, only slightly less important, include the strength of the parent material for the gravel, earth, and sand; the on-site control of mixing and wetting; and the degree of care taken in placing and compacting the material in the forms. The concerns of the earth builder, in short, include all the concerns of the concrete builder.

As a general rule, unreinforced wall dimensions should be constrained by height-to-width ratios such as those published in the Uniform Code for Building Conservation (UCBC, Table A-1-G) for stone and adobe walls:

	SEISMIC ZONE		
	2B	3	4
One-story buildings	12	10	8
Two-story buildings			
first story	14	11	9
second story	12	10	8

These values will usually provide ample latitude to the designer. Earth walls are by their nature massive — wall widths are often governed by the design of formwork and the ability of workers to place and compact the mix. Although a nine-foot-high wall could theoretically be as narrow as 11 or 12 inches, 16 or 18 inches may be the minimum to allow access to the bottom of the form, even with an extended pneumatic tamper. (Gunearth could theoretically be thinner than rammed earth, and can even be applied as a thin surfacing material. But as a structural wall, gunearth should generally be as thick or nearly as thick as its rammed counterpart because, using exactly the same mix design, gunearth is less strong than rammed earth.) Furthermore, if there are any rebar, conduit, plumbing, or other inserts in the formwork, the minimum width gets even bigger, both for access and to ensure a thick enough covering over embedments to prevent cracking. Wall widths of 16, 18, and 24 inches are common, and wider or battered (tapered) walls are also possible.

Design in Seismic Areas

In seismically active areas, the nature of the design changes radically. Earthquake forces are in direct proportion to mass, so the load on heavy earth-walled structures is acute. Portland cement must be added, generally at about one to three sacks per cubic yard (4 to 12 percent cement by volume); the wall must have steel reinforcing; and it is essential to know the material strength of the specific project mix.

(Having made these assertions, I must also admit and point out the existence of historical buildings that by their survival suggest otherwise. In particular, David Easton's investigation of the 130-year-old Chew Kee store, a rammed earth structure built by Chinese immigrants in the Sacramento Valley of California and documented in *The Rammed Earth House*, revealed very solid walls that had no foundations at all and had endured fire, earthquake, constant occupancy, rain, and freezes with remarkably little damage. Nevertheless, California, China, Iran, and other seismically active parts of the world have their many sad stories of lives lost in collapsing rammed earth or adobe buildings. Although the types of earth construction discussed here are inherently stronger than the old adobes, our level of understanding, particularly with regard to earthquakes, is only partial. We do know that proper design and moisture protection is far more important than material strength for the longevity of earthen structures. But until we know far more than we currently do about stabilized earth design and construction, an extra level of caution in seismic earth wall design seems warranted.)

Foundations

The foundation for an earth-walled building must be particularly stout to span soft spots in the ground and prevent settling cracks in the comparatively brittle wall. If the walls need to cantilever off the foundation under wind or earthquake loads, then the footing must be wide enough to provide a stable base and not overstress the soil.

Bond Beams

The weight of the roof, and sometimes floors, must be borne at the top of the earth wall. Standard practice is to provide some sort of bond (or tie) beam along the top of the wall. The bond beam serves to receive and evenly distribute the weight of the supported structure and tie together the tops of walls, in a manner analogous to the strapping around packing crates.

Lateral Loads

Wind loads and in-plane shearing loads are rarely excessive for earth walls, although narrow piers and/or large openings in a wall will create stress concentrations and should be carefully reviewed.

In designing an earth wall for in-plane forces, the following factors are important for avoiding cracking, and can be adjusted in relation to each other:

- The strength of the stabilized earth material.
- The thickness of the wall — shear stresses generally decrease with increasing thickness.
- The presence (or lack) of steel reinforcing. Somewhat like poured concrete, a grid of horizontal and vertical bars can be placed in the wall; by keeping the bar spacing tight, usually no more than 12 or 16 inches vertically and horizontally, there usually will be several bars spanning across any potential tension crack in the wall.

Referring back to Part One's discussion of earthquakes and top restraint for an earth wall in a seismically active area: the connection plates, bolts, and straps must be carefully designed and the floor or roof itself designed to be able to act as a stiff diaphragm capable of transmitting the reaction (which can be on the order of 1,000 pounds per foot) to the supporting crosswalls. Though generally feasible, especially for small buildings, this approach will add extensive structure to the ceiling and cost to the job.

The alternative, again, is to consider that the wall is fixed (cantilevered) at the foundation and free at the top, with the footing made wide enough to stabilize the wall against overturning. If the foundation is on drilled piers, the piers will have to stagger around the wall centerline to give stability to the footing. The supported roof or floor is then considered to "float" on the walls, which are self-supporting in an earthquake (and are thus allowed, in the UBC, a one-third reduction in design loads).

In either case, crosswalls of the same construction (or something else of comparable strength and stiffness, such as plywood-sheathed wood stud walls), can be tied to the supported wall and the foundation so as to comprise vertical lines of support for the earth wall.

Analysis Method

To date, engineers in California have been adapting the working stress method of design for masonry walls (or "Alternate Design Method" for concrete as defined in the UBC) for use in designing stabilized earth walls. Allowable stresses in the earth wall are defined as a function of the material's ultimate compressive strength f'_c (f'_m in masonry), as follows:[1]

- allowable shear stress in wall — $F_v = 1.0 \times \sqrt{f'_c}$
- allowable flexural compressive stress in wall — $F_b = 0.45\ f'_c$
- allowable axial compressive stress in wall — $F_a = 0.2\ f'_c$
- allowable bearing stress in wall — $F_{br} = 0.3\ f'_c$
- modulus of elasticity — $E_m = 750\ f'_c$
- allowable tensile stress in deformed bars — $F_s = 20,000$ psi (for grade 40 bars)
- allowable bond stress in deformed bars[2] — $u = 140$ psi

Because, as with concrete, most calculations are based on f'_c, it is essential to establish as accurately as possible the material's compressive strength. Again, given the wide variety of soil types, theoretical prediction is difficult. Where strength considerations are really important, as in seismically active areas, the designer should generate job-specific mixes to be sampled, cured, and tested before final analysis. Test specimens can be tamped (quasi-rammed) into standard six-inch test cylinders, but this may not yield as reliable results as taking drilled cores from a small section of test wall. (Building a section of test wall also affords an opportunity to test construction methods, train workers, and provide color samples to the owner.)

1   Some values have been simplified for this presentation and will vary somewhat depending on stress combinations, wall geometry, and reinforcing properties.
2   The value for bond stress will probably vary; see previous discussion on test results for gunearth and ensuing discussion of bond strength for rammed earth.

Having established the strength of the mix, most designers will then use one-half of the established f'_c (akin to assuming uninspected masonry) to generate other working stresses (but use full f'_c to calculate E_m). If there will be little site control, or if there has been no testing program, substantially lesser values might be used, such as $1/4\, f'_c$ or even $1/8\, f'_c$, depending on the occupancy importance (potential hazard) and the designer's judgment. Under lateral loads of wind and earthquake, the code allows a 33 percent allowable stress increase (because, just like you and I, most materials can handle an occasional 33 percent stress increase as long as it doesn't last too long or happen too often).

DESIGN AND CONSTRUCTION CONSIDERATIONS

Stabilized Earth

With such massive walls, the design is governed by gravity loads: dead loads (predominantly the wall itself, generally about 110 to 140 pounds per cubic foot) and live loads. Wind loading on one- or two-story buildings is rarely problematic, so empirical design, based on centuries of experience, should be adequate in most cases. Besides limiting the height-to-width ratios, wall lengths and size/location of openings should be constrained. Here, rules of thumb can be borrowed from unreinforced masonry construction:

- Limit the total length of openings along the wall to one-third of the total wall length (or a larger fraction if the wall is reinforced).
- Provide horizontal reinforcing or lintels over openings, extending at least 24 inches past the sides of the openings.
- Limit the proportions of piers; they should not get too tall and narrow. In particular, the corner piers at the ends of the wall should have a height no more than four times the width and be at least four feet wide.

Deviations from these geometrical guidelines, i.e., from the empirical rules handed down by experience, should only be made if an engineer calculates and approves the alternative configuration.

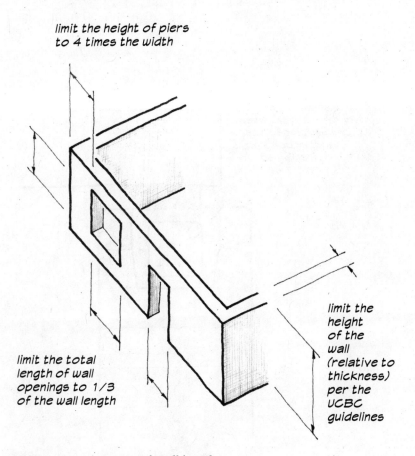

limit the height of piers to 4 times the width

limit the total length of wall openings to 1/3 of the wall length

limit the height of the wall (relative to thickness) per the UCBC guidelines

FIGURE 19. *openings and wall lengths*

Rammed Earth

The bond beam on a rammed wall can be wood — various lapped, nailed, screwed, or strapped combinations of lumber and plywood. A more effective bond beam, however, is made of reinforced concrete, by laying rebar along the top of the last lift and pouring concrete into the tops of the forms. To keep finish wall colors similar, the bond beam might be a similar mix to the wall below, with more cement and water for strength and pourability. However, the presence of any appreciable soil (clay) in the mix will inevitably lead to additional cracking; if the

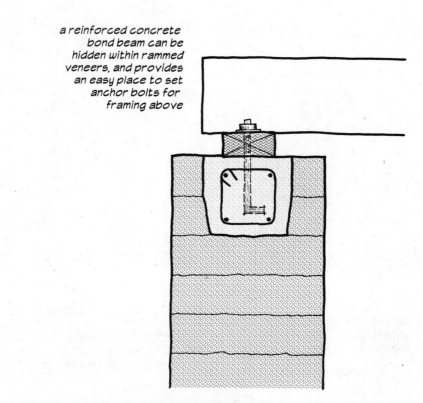

*a reinforced concrete
bond beam can be
hidden within rammed
veneers, and provides
an easy place to set
anchor bolts for
framing above*

FIGURE 20. *rammed earth bond beam*

bond beam's performance is crucial, regular reinforced concrete should be used. The bond beam should be at least six inches thick and have a sill plate to receive roof and/or floor structure.

Door and window formwork must be stout enough to take the load of ramming, and openings must be spanned by a permanent wood, steel, or concrete lintel designed for the weight above. (Restrictions in the UBC regarding the use of wood to support concrete or masonry apply here; the use of wood as a lintel, or as a bond beam in seismic zones 3 and 4, is prohibited.) Horizontal reinforcing can be laid into the lift above the opening to act as an integral lintel.

Design of steel reinforcing, when used, must be conservative, for here the similarity between rammed earth and poured concrete construction is uncertain. Of concern is the bond strength — the amount of grab between the surface of the reinforcing bar and the surrounding rammed earth. Without a firm bond, the rebar is not an integral part of the earth wall, and cannot fully provide the intended reinforcing, particularly across a tension crack.

A recent laboratory pullout test of a horizontal rebar in a rammed wall gave a bond strength of 380 psi, which is higher than a working stress analysis or code might predict or allow. This is not so surprising, as the process of ramming mechanically packs material against and around the bar. However, the vertical bars have less of this advantage, and may in fact have diminished bond from being inadvertently jostled during ramming. Finally, the aesthetic nature of earth walls is such that the desired look is often one of sloping, irregular, and/or curving strata (lifts), as opposed to even, horizontal bands. In such cases, the layout, placement, and bond of horizontal bars requires special attention. In all cases, the amount and location of reinforcing in the wall must be designed so as not to interfere with the ramming process. Vertical bars are wired to foundation dowels, but horizontal bars can be set in place between lifts as the work progresses.

Gunearth

The bond beam in a gunned wall can simply be a rebar cage wired into the wall top. Or, as is the case with rammed earth, the bond beam can be reinforced concrete connected to the wall by means of the wall reinforcing. In all cases, a wood sill plate with anchor bolts will be necessary to attach the supported floor or roof.

Formwork for gunearth walls is only one-sided (some are even experimenting with formless systems shot from both sides and using expanded metal lath attached to the rebar grid to catch and hold the shot material), and can be troweled, screeded, or left with its native "cottage cheese" surface. It will show more shrinkage cracking than concrete or gunite (because of the clay content), so the addition of crack-restraining plastic or straw fibers is good practice.

Door and window openings need only be simple blockouts with lintel reinforcing over the top. In seismic zones 3 and 4, reinforcing should be installed on all sides of openings and extended past the openings, so as to contain the diagonal cracks illustrated earlier.

UBC code provisions for gunite and shotcrete generally apply to gunearth. Reinforcing splices should be specially wired to avoid shadowing (voids behind rebar), and experienced mixers and nozzle handlers are crucial for an effective installation. Reinforcing bond strength is generally higher than with rammed earth because the bars aren't being jostled by ramming activity, the mix is wetter, and the material is applied forcefully onto the rebar surface. As with gunite, there is extensive rebound waste (generally 10 to 20 percent), so provision must be made for disposing of the material left on the ground, preferably by using it for a ground slab or by packing it immediately into forms for site pavers.

SAMPLE CALCULATIONS

Following are three sample calculations for the same wall in three different conditions. Though presented as simply as possible, some of this will inevitably be comprehensible only to structural engineers, and is intended for their reference in generating their own earth wall analyses.

Note — for simplification, two considerations important to the calculations have been neglected: 1) the added in-plane seismic load from supported crosswalls, and 2) the diminished structural wall length due to window and door openings (see discussion of *piers* in Part One). Although a full, three-dimensional building design is beyond the scope of this book, any actual building design must account for these and other project-specific factors.

In each of the three sample calculations, the problem is to design a 16-inch-thick wall, 9 feet high from foundation to plate. Tests have shown f'_c to be at least 800 psi. Total imposed loads from the supported roof are 300 pounds per linear foot, applied at the wall centerline, and the finish material weighs 120 pcf.

Case 1: Seismic zone 2B (a non-earthquake-prone area)

■ check h/t ratio

(9 x 12) / 16 = 6.75 < 12 allowed — OK

■ axial compressive stress at top of footing

f_a = (roof weight of 300 pounds divided by the wall width of 1.33') + (weight of a 1' x 1' x 9' column of earth wall @ 120 pcf) divided by 144 (square inches per square foot = (300 / 1.33 + (9 x 120 pcf)) / 144 = 1,305 / 144 = 9 psi

allowable axial compressive stress
F_a = 0.2 (f'$_c$/2) = 0.2 (800/2) = 80 psi > 9 calculated — OK

If wall openings are constrained as described, and have lintels, the wall is OK, with no reinforcing, by empirical analysis.

Case 2: Seismic zone 4 (an earthquake-prone area), wall cantilevered

■ check h/t ratio

6.75 < 8 allowed — OK

■ horizontal earthquake load

F_p = $^2/_3$ $ZI_pC_pW_p$
- $^2/_3$ modifier for wall cantilevered at base is allowed by UBC
- Z = 0.4 = coefficient for seismic zone 4 (area of highest risk, as in coastal California)
- I_p = 1.0 = coefficient for occupancy importance (this is higher for hospitals, schools, fire stations, etc.)

- C_p = 0.75 = structure coefficient for type of load-resisting system (in this case, a massive, rigid "concrete" shear wall system)
- W_p = the structure dead load = 1' x 1.33' x 120 pcf = 160 pounds per foot

(For simplicity's sake, we will neglect in this example the dead load of the roof, which would be an additional horizontal force at the top of the wall.)

F_p = ($2/3$ x 0.4 x 1.0 x 0.75) W_p = 0.2 W_p
    = 0.2 (1.33' x 120 plf) = 32 lbs/vertical foot

design moment M = 32 lbs/ft x 9' x 9' / 2 = 1,296 ft-lbs
    = 15,552 in-lbs per foot of wall

design shear V = 32 lbs/ft x 9' = 288 lbs per foot of wall

Try #4 grade 40 bars @ 12" oc each way in wall centerline (area of steel reinforcing A_s = 0.20 in^2 per foot of wall).

design f_c = $f'_c/2$ = 800/2 = 400 psi
- n = modular ratio = E_{steel} / E_{earth} = 29 x 10^6 / (750 x 800) = 48
- d = depth to reinforcing from compression face = half wall thickness = 8"
- p = ratio of reinforcing steel area to compression area = 0.20 / (12 x 8) = .0021 in^2 / ft
- np = .101   k = .3597   j = .8801
  (k and j are arithmetical values derived from the quantity np; k = $\sqrt{[(2np) + (np)^2]}$ - np, and j = 1 - (k/3).

■ compressive bending stress

f_b = 2M / $kjbd^2$ = 2 x 15,552) / (.3597 x .8801 x 12 x 8^2) = 128 psi

allowable bending stress
    F_b = 0.45 f_c = 0.45 x 400 x 1.33 = 239 psi > 128 — OK

■ shear stress

f_v = V / bjd = 288 / 12 x .8801 x 8 = 4 psi

allowable shear stress
$$F_v = 1.0 \ \sqrt{f}\ '_c \ x\ 1.33 = 1.0\ x\ \sqrt{400}\ x\ 1.33 = 27\ psi > 4 — OK$$

■ tensile bending stress in reinforcing

f_s = M / $A_s$jd = 15,552 / 0.20 x .8801 x 8 = 11,044 psi

allowable tensile stress F_s = 20,000 psi > 11,044 — OK

Case 3: Seismic zone 4, same wall restrained at top

■ horizontal earthquake load

F_p = (32 lbs/vertical foot) / $^2/_3$ = 48 lbs/vertical foot

(2/3 modifier for cantilevered wall does not apply to wall restrained at top.)

design moment M = 48 x 9^2 / 8 = 486 ft-lbs = 5,832 in-lbs

design shear V = 48 x 9 / 2 = 216 lbs

Try #4 grade 40 bars @ 16'' oc each way in wall centerline (A_s = 0.20 / 1.33 = 0.15 in^2 per foot of wall length).

■ design f_c

f_c = 1/2 f'_c = 400 psi   n = 48   d = 8''

p = 0.15/(12 x 8) = .0016   np = .075   k = .3194   j = .8935

■ **compressive bending stress**

f_b = 2M / kjbd^2 = 53 psi < 239 psi allowable — OK

■ **shear stress**

f_v = V / bjd = 3 psi < 27 psi allowable — OK

■ **tensile bending stress in reinforcing**

f_s = M/A$_s$jd = 5,439 psi < 20,000 psi — OK

■ **wall connection at top**

reaction at top = shear V = 216 pounds per foot

Design wall connection at top for (2 x 216) = 432 pounds per foot.

CONCLUSIONS

The abundance of historic and modern earth-walled structures around the world gives us some empirical basis for design of new buildings, and a fair amount of testing to date has increased our understanding of soil-cement. Though not yet specifically defined or acknowledged in the major building codes, stabilized earth construction can now be described, specified, and analyzed in a rational way as allowed in the alternative materials provisions of the major codes. Where large seismic forces are probable, the analysis must be cautious, and strength assumptions based on a verifiable testing program, but earth walls can certainly be designed to meet code requirements for life safety.

A structural "wish list" for future testing programs includes:

- a full-scale shake table test of wall assemblies under dynamic loading
- a thorough exploration of bond stress, particularly in rammed earth

- development of an easy, accurate field test to determine usefulness (anticipated strength) of site soils for wall material
- development of curves showing compressive strength versus cure time

As is the case with every other building material, those of us in the building and engineering community will continue refining our understanding as more and more stabilized earth projects are completed and more testing is done. We hope the day will soon come when modern building codes recognize earth wall construction and provide chapters to define and guide safe practice.

APPENDIX E-1: SOIL REFERENCES

Clay Size	Silt Size		Fine Sand	Medium Sand	Coarse Sand	Fine Gravel	Coarse Gravel	Cobbles[2]	Unified Soil Classification ASTM D2487 (FAA, US-DOD, USBR, TVA)
Fines (Clay and Silt)[1]									
Silt Clay (combined silt and clay)			Fine Sand	Coarse Sand		Gravel		Boulders	AASHTO Soil Classification AASHTO N-145
Colloids[3]	Clay	Silt	Fine Sand	Coarse Sand	Fine Gravel	Medium Gravel	Coarse Gravel	Boulders	AASHTO Soil-Aggregate AASHTO N-146
Clay		Silt	Fine Sand	Coarse Sand	Fine Gravel		Coarse Gravel		U.S. Dept. of Agriculture Soil Classification
Clay Size	Silt Size		Fine Sand	Coarse Sand		Gravel			Prior FAA Soil Classification (Unified system is in current use)
	Clay and Silt								
Clay	Fine Silt	Medium Silt	Coarse Silt	Fine Sand	Medium Sand	Coarse Sand	Fine Gravel	Medium Gravel / Coarse Gravel	British Standard BS1377

Sieve Size / Particle Size, mm

[1]Clay: PI≥4 and plot of PI vs. LL falls above "A" line in Table 4.
Silt: PI<4 or plot of PI vs. LL falls below "A" line in Table 4.
[2]Boulders are particles retained on a 12-in. square opening sieve.
[3]Colloids are part of the clay fraction.

FIGURE 21. *soil size gradations*
(reprinted from PCA Soil Primer, *figure 1)*

General classification	Granular materials (35% or less passing No. 200)							Silt-clay materials (More than 35% passing No. 200)			
	A-1		A-3	A-2				A-4	A-5	A-6	A-7
Group classification	A-1-a	A-1-b		A-2-4	A-2-5	A-2-6	A-2-7				A-7-5 A-7-6
Sieve analysis, percent passing:											
No. 10	50 max.	—	—	—	—	—	—	—	—	—	—
No. 40	30 max.	50 max.	51 min.	—	—	—	—	—	—	—	—
No. 200	15 max.	25 max.	10 max.	35 max.	35 max.	35 max.	35 max.	36 min.	36 min.	36 min.	36 min.
Characteristics of fraction passing No. 40:											
Liquid limit	—		—	40 max.	41 min.	40 max.	41 min.	40 max.	41 min.	40 max.	41 min.
Plasticity index	6 max.		NP	10 max.	10 max.	11 min.	11 min.	10 max.	10 max.	11 min.	11 min.*
Usual types of significant constituent materials	Stone fragments, gravel and sand		Fine sand	Silty or clayey gravel and sand				Silty soils		Clayey soils	
General rating as subgrade	Excellent to good							Fair to poor			

*Plasticity index of A-7-5 subgroup is equal to or less than LL minus 30. Plasticity index of A-7-6 subgroup is greater than LL minus 30.

FIGURE 22. *AASHTO soil classifications*
(reprinted from PCA Soil Primer, *table 3)*

APPENDIX E-2: SOIL-CEMENT REFERENCES

Typical cement requirements for various soil types

AASHTO soil classification	ASTM soil classification	Typical range of cement requirement,* percent by weight	Typical cement content for moisture-density test (ASTM D 558), percent by weight	Typical cement contents for durability tests (ASTM D 559 and D 506), percent by weight
A-1-a	GW, GP, GM, SW, SP, SM	3-5	5	3-5-7
A-1-b	GM, GP, SM, SP	5-8	6	4-6-8
A-2	GM, GC, SM, SC	5-9	7	5-7-9
A-3	SP	7-11	9	7-9-11
A-4	CL, ML	7-12	10	8-10-12
A-5	ML, MH, CH	8-13	10	8-10-12
A-6	CL, CH	9-15	12	10-12-14
A-7	MH, CH	10-16	13	11-13-15

*Does not include organic or poorly reacting soils. Also, additional cement may be required for severe exposure conditions such as slope protection.

FIGURE 23. *typical cement requirements for various soil types (reprinted from ACI 230.1R-90, table 3.1)*

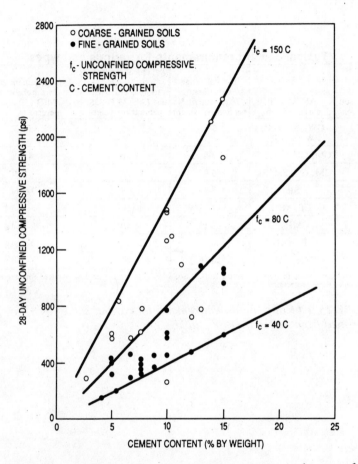

FIGURE 24. *relationship between cement content and unconfined compressive strength for soil-cement mixtures (reprinted from ACI 230.1R-90, figure 4.2)*

APPENDIX E-3: SAMPLE SPECIFICATION

Note: this is adapted from a very large, complex job in a high seismic risk area, involving "museum quality" finishes; most stabilized earth projects would not be so exacting.

SECTION 03900 - CEMENT-STABILIZED EARTH (SE)

PART 1 - GENERAL

1.1 RELATED DOCUMENTS

A. Permit Drawings

1.2 SUMMARY

A. This Section specifies stabilized earth, including formwork, reinforcing, mix design, placement procedures, and finishes.

B. Stabilized earth includes the following:

1. Gunearth walls
2. Gunearth veneer
3. Rammed earth walls
4. Rammed earth columns

1.3 SUBMITTALS

A. General: Submit laboratory test reports for stabilized earth materials and mix design test to the structural engineer and building inspector for review prior to construction.

1.4 QUALITY ASSURANCE

A. Concrete Testing Service: Engage a testing agency acceptable to Architect to perform material evaluation tests and to design mixes.

B. Materials and installed work may require testing and retesting at any time during progress of Work. Tests, including retesting of rejected materials for installed Work, shall be done at Contractor's expense.

PART 2 - PRODUCTS

2.1 FORM MATERIALS

A. Forms for exposed finish stabilized earth: Plywood, metal, or other acceptable panel-type materials to provide continuous, straight, smooth, exposed surfaces. Furnish in largest practicable sizes to minimize number of joints and to conform to joint system shown on drawings.

1. Use overlaid plywood complying with U.S. Product Standard PS-1 "A-C or B-B High Density Overlaid Concrete Form," Class I.

B. Forms for unexposed finish stabilized earth: plywood, lumber, metal, or another acceptable material. Provide lumber dressed on at least two edges and one side for tight fit.

C. Form release agent: provide commercial formulation form release agent with a maximum of 350 g/L volatile organic compounds (VOCs) that will not bond with, stain, or adversely affect stabilized earth surfaces and will not impair subsequent treatments of surfaces.

D. Form ties: factory-fabricated, adjustable-length, removable or snap-off metal form ties designed to prevent form deflection and to prevent spalling of stabilized earth upon removal. Provide units that will leave no metal closer than $1 \frac{1}{2}$ inches to the plane of the exposed surface.

2.2 REINFORCING MATERIALS

A. Reinforcing Bars:

1. #6 and larger: ASTM A 615, Grade 60, deformed.

2. #5 and smaller: ASTM A 615, Grade 40, deformed.

B. Mesh (for gunearth veneer): 17 gauge galvanized stucco mesh.

2.3 STABILIZED EARTH MATERIALS

A. Portland Cement: ASTM C 150, Type I or II.

1. Use one brand of cement for each color (gray, tan, and white) throughout Project unless otherwise acceptable to Architect.

B. Earth: Red Nun's Canyon fines from the Nun's Canyon Quarry in Glen Ellen, with maximum aggregate size $\frac{3}{8}$ inch, a maximum of 20% passing a #200 sieve, plastic limit of 21, liquid limit of 30, pH of 4.0, and a plasticity index of 9. All earth used shall have values within 10% +/- of the above.

C. Water: Potable.

D. Sand: free of salts, organic materials, or other contaminants.

E. Fiber reinforcement: Polypropylene fibers engineered and designed for secondary reinforcement of stabilized earth work, complying with ASTM C 1116, Type III, not less than $^3/_4$ inch long.

2.4 RELATED MATERIALS

A. Reglets: Where sheet flashing or bituminous membranes are terminated in reglets, provide reglets of not less than 0.0217-inch-thick (26-gage) galvanized or stainless sheet steel or copper. Fill reglet or cover face opening to prevent intrusion of stabilized earth or debris.

B. Dovetail Anchor Slots: Hot-dip galvanized or stainless sheet steel or copper, not less than 0.0336 inch thick (22 gage) with bent tab anchors. Fill slot with temporary filler or cover face opening to prevent intrusion of stabilized earth or debris.

C. Absorptive Cover: Burlap cloth made from jute or kenaf, weighing approximately 9 oz. per sq. yd., complying with AASHTO M 182, Class 2.

D. Moisture-Retaining Cover: One of the following, complying with ASTM C-171.

    1. Waterproof paper.

    2. Polyethylene film.

    3. Polyethylene-coated burlap.

E. Epoxy Adhesive: ASTM C 881, two-component material suitable for use on dry or damp surfaces. Provide material type, grade, and class to suit Project requirements.

2.5 PROPORTIONING AND DESIGNING MIXES

A. Following are the mixes for each type of stabilized earth:

    1. Gunearth: Add water at the nozzle as required for complete mixing and hydration, but not so much as to permit the emplaced material to slump. Basic "721": 70% Red Nun's Canyon fines (NCF), 20% Olympia II sand, and 10% Colton cement.

    2. Rammed earth: Add water at about 13% of the dry mix weight (this is the amount that, when added and mixed, will give a material consistency that can be balled up in the hand, dropped from waist height, and will break into several coher-

ent clods (neither shattering nor "splatting"), i.e., the universally recognized hand-drop test for moisturizing rammed earth.)

 a. Lightest Color: 68% NCF, 20% Oly sand, 12% white cement.

 b. Medium Light Color: 72% NCF, 10% Oly sand, 10% Delta fill sand, 8% Colton Block cement.

 c. Medium Dark Color: 69% NCF, 20% Delta fill sand, 8% Colton Block cement, 3% gray cement.

 d. Darkest Color: 72% NCF, 20% Delta fill sand, 8% gray cement.

B. Mixes of stabilized earth are designed to attain, at a minimum:

 1. Rammed earth: 2500-psi, 56-day compressive strength.

 2. Gunearth: 1600-psi, 56-day compressive strength.

C. Adjustment to stabilized earth mixes: Mix design adjustments may be requested by Contractor when characteristics of materials, job conditions, weather, test results, or other circumstances warrant, as accepted by Architect. Laboratory test data for revised mix design and strength results must be submitted to and accepted by Architect before using in Work.

D. Fiber Reinforcement: Add at manufacturer's recommended rate to all mixes but not less than 1.5 lb per cu. yd.

2.6 STABILIZED EARTH MIXING

A. Gunearth: using gunite mixing drums and hoppers as modified for pneumatically applied stabilized earth.

B. Rammed earth: using a mechanically powered rotary mixer on a clean, dry surface onsite, kept continuously clean of extraneous debris and partially cured cement-stabilized earth. Material shall be placed and rammed within 1.5 hours of wetting or shall be discarded.

PART 3 - EXECUTION

3.1 GENERAL

A. Coordinate the installation of joint materials, conduit, junction boxes, and other related materials with placement of forms and reinforcing steel.

3.2 FORMS

A. General: Design, erect, support, brace, and maintain formwork to support vertical, lateral, static, and dynamic loads that might be applied until stabilized earth structure can support such loads. Construct formwork so stabilized earth members and structures are of correct size, shape, alignment, elevation, and position. Maintain formwork construction tolerances and surface irregularities complying with the following ACI 347 limits:

　　1. Provide Class A tolerances for surfaces exposed to view.

　　2. Provide Class C tolerances for other surfaces.

B. Construct forms to sizes, shapes, lines, and dimensions shown and to obtain accurate alignment, location, grades, level, and plumb work in finished structures. Provide for openings, offsets, sinkages, keyways, recesses, moldings, rustications, reglets, chamfers, blocking, screeds, bulkheads, anchorages and inserts, and other features required in the Work. Use selected materials to obtain required finishes. Solidly butt joints and provide backup at joints to prevent form lines at exposed surfaces.

C. Fabricate forms for easy removal without hammering or prying against surfaces. Provide crush plates or wrecking plates where stripping may damage stabilized earth surfaces. Shape wood inserts to form keyways, reglets, recesses, and the like for easy removal.

D. Chamfer exposed corners and edges as indicated, using wood, metal, PVC, or rubber chamfer strips fabricated to produce uniform smooth lines and tight edge joints.

E. Provisions for Other Trades: Provide openings in stabilized earth formwork to accommodate work of other trades. Determine size and location of openings, recesses, and chases from trades providing such items. Accurately place and securely support items built into forms.

F. Cleaning and Tightening: Thoroughly clean forms and adjacent surfaces to receive stabilized earth. Remove chips, wood, sawdust, dirt, or other debris just before placing stabilized earth. Retighten forms and bracing before placing stabilized earth, as required, to maintain proper alignment.

3.3 PLACING REINFORCEMENT

A. General: Comply with Concrete Reinforcing Steel Institute's recommended practice for "Placing Reinforcing Bars," for details and methods of reinforcement placement and supports and as specified.

B. Clean reinforcement of loose rust and mill scale, earth, ice, and other materials that reduce or destroy bond with stabilized earth.

C. Accurately position, support, and secure reinforcement against displacement. Locate and support reinforcing by metal chairs, runners, bolsters, spacers, and hangers, as approved by Architect. Horizontal reinforcing in rammed earth, except as noted, shall be placed in forms, without ties, between lifts.

D. Place reinforcement to maintain minimum coverages as indicated for stabilized earth protection. Arrange, space, and securely tie bars and bar supports to hold reinforcement in position during stabilized earth placement operations. Set wire ties so ends are directed into stabilized earth, not toward exposed surfaces.

E. Install stucco mesh for veneer in lengths as long as practicable. Lap adjoining pieces at least five full mesh spaces and lace splices with wire. Offset laps of adjoining widths to prevent continuous laps in either direction.

3.4 JOINTS

A. Construction Joints: Locate and install construction joints so they do not impair strength or appearance of the structure, as acceptable to Architect.

B. For any rammed earth lift that will not receive the next lift within 2 hours, thoroughly roughen the exposed surface. Such joints in walls shall also slope to the outside at a pitch of 3 to 12.

C. Continue reinforcement across construction joints except as indicated otherwise.

3.5 INSTALLING EMBEDDED ITEMS

A. General: Set and build into formwork anchorage devices and other embedded items required for other work that is attached to or supported by stabilized earth. Use setting drawings, diagrams, instructions, and directions provided by suppliers of items to be attached.

B. Install reglets to receive top edge of foundation sheet water-proofing and to receive through-wall flashings in outer face of stabilized earth at exterior walls, where flashing is shown at lintels, relieving angles, and other conditions.

3.6 STABILIZED EARTH PLACEMENT

A. Inspection: Before placing stabilized earth, inspect and complete formwork installation, reinforcing steel, and items to be embedded or cast in. Notify other trades to permit installation of their work.

B. Build rammed earth in layers of 6 inch maximum finish thickness, compacted to 92% minimum Proctor Density. For any rammed earth lift that will not receive the next lift within 2 hours, thoroughly roughen the exposed surface (except top lifts). Such joints in walls shall also slope to the outside at a pitch of 3 to 12.

D. Placing Gunearth: Deposit material in a manner to avoid inclined construction joints. Where placement consists of several layers, place each layer while preceding layer is still plastic to avoid cold joints.

E. Cold-Weather Placement: Comply with provisions of ACI 306 and as follows. Protect stabilized earth work from physical damage or reduced strength that could be caused by frost, freezing actions, or low temperatures.

F. When air temperature has fallen to or is expected to fall below 40 deg F (4 deg C), uniformly heat water and aggregates before mixing to obtain a stabilized earth mixture temperature of not less than 50 deg F (10 deg C) and not more than 80 deg F (27 deg C) at point of placement.

   1. Do not use calcium chloride, salt, or other materials containing antifreeze agents or chemical accelerators unless otherwise accepted in mix designs.

G. Hot-Weather Placement:

1. Cover reinforcing steel with water-soaked burlap if it becomes too hot, so that steel temperature will not exceed the ambient air temperature immediately before embedding in stabilized earth.

2. Fog spray forms and reinforcing steel just before placing stabilized earth.

3.7 STABILIZED EARTH PERSONNEL

A. Provide names and experience records of nozzlemen and ramming crew foremen for approval by Engineer prior to work; keep these names available onsite. At all times during any stabilized earth work, at least one member of the stabilized earth crew fluent in the language of any workers and that of the Contractor shall be onsite for coordination with Contractor.

3.8 STABILIZED EARTH CURING AND PROTECTION

A. General: Protect freshly placed stabilized earth from premature drying and excessive cold or hot temperatures. (Moisture curing, as is typically used for reinforced concrete, has been found to exacerbate efflorescence, and should not be done unless directed by Architect in writing.)

3.9 REMOVING FORMS

A. General: Formwork *not* supporting weight of stabilized earth, such as sides of beams, walls, columns, and similar parts of the work, may be removed after cumulatively curing at not less than 50 deg F (10 deg C) for 24 hours after placing material, provided stabilized earth is sufficiently hard to not be damaged by form-removal operations, and provided curing and protection operations are maintained.

3.10 REUSING FORMS

A. Clean and repair surfaces of forms to be reused in the Work. Split, frayed, delaminated, or otherwise damaged form-facing material will not be acceptable for exposed surfaces. Apply new form-coating compound as specified for new formwork.

B. When forms are extended for successive stabilized earth placement, thoroughly clean surfaces, remove fins and laitance, and tighten forms to close joints. Align and secure joints to avoid offsets. Do not use patched forms for exposed surfaces except as acceptable to Architect.

3.11 QUALITY CONTROL TESTING DURING CONSTRUCTION

A. General: The Contractor will employ a testing agency to perform tests and to submit test reports.

B. Sampling and testing for quality control during stabilized earth placement includes the following, or as directed by Engineer.

1. Conduct compressive strength tests per ASTM C 39 on the following:

a. Compression test cylinders complying with ASTM C 31 for rammed earth. Mold and cure cylinders out of direct sunlight.

b. 3-inch drilled cores complying with ASTM C 42, taken from gunearth panels 18' x 18' x 5.5" thick, cured out of direct sunlight.

2. Test program is two-phased as follows:

a. Phase One: for each day's work, obtain 12 test specimens of each of the four rammed earth mixes, and of the gunearth mix. For each of these five mixes, test 6 specimens at 14 days, 3 at 28 days, and 2 at 56 days (hold the last specimen). Phase One continues until, for each of the five mixes, 36 specimens have been cast.

b. Phase Two: for each day's work, obtain 4 test specimens of each of the four rammed earth mixes, and of the gunearth mix. For each of these five mixes, test 2 specimens at 14 days, 1 at 28 days, and 1 at 56 days.

3. Results of Phase One accelerated testing will be used to develop curves for each mix relating early age to percent of 56-day design strength. Criteria for satisfactory 14- and 28-day strengths will then be established.

4. Strength level of stabilized earth will be considered satisfactory if averages of sets of three consecutive 56-day strength test results equal or exceed specified compressive strength and

no individual strength test result falls below specified compressive strength by more than 500 psi.

C. Test results will be reported in writing to Architect, Structural Engineer, and Contractor within 24 hours after tests. Reports of compressive strength tests shall contain the Project identification name and number, name of testing service, date of stabilized earth placement, stabilized earth type and class, location of batch in structure, design compressive strength at 56 days, and specimen compressive breaking strength.

D. Additional Tests: The testing agency will make additional tests of in-place stabilized earth when test results indicate specified strengths have not been attained in the structure, as directed by Engineer. Testing agency may conduct tests to determine adequacy of stabilized earth by cored cylinders complying with ASTM C 42, or by other methods as directed.

END OF SECTION 03900

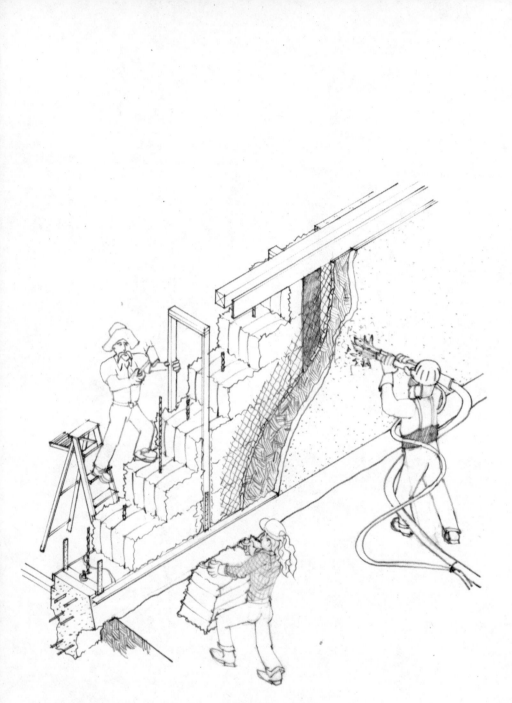

straw-bale wall
Courtesy of David Arkin, Arkin-Tilt Architects

part three

STRAW

Coming back —
so many pathways
through the spring grass.

— Buson

The first known straw-bale structures were built about a hundred
years ago by European and New Englander settlers in the Sand Hills of
western Nebraska. Having little other means to shelter themselves —
almost no lumber or stone, and a lesser quality of sod than was used
elsewhere on the plains — they were driven by necessity to improvise.
Using the newly invented mechanical baling machines, they baled the
grasses that surrounded them, stacked the bales to form walls, and
applied mud or cement plasters inside and out. Some of those homes
still exist, and are still in good shape, as are a few others built over the
subsequent few decades throughout the West. A revival in straw-bale

FIGURE 25. *older straw-bale structure — Pilgrim Holiness Church,
Arthur, Nebraska*

construction began in the American West in the 1970s, propelled largely by owner-builders with an interest in sustainable building and lifestyle. Although a wider variety of grain straws are now used, and balers and construction techniques are now more sophisticated, the basics of straw-bale construction remain very much the same.

Straw bales have now been used in construction all over the world and in an ingenious variety of ways. Although domes, arches, curved walls, multistory homes, and large-scale buildings such as warehouses and barns have now been built, or attempted, the vast majority of straw-bale buildings are homes with simple, one-story rectangular plans and pitched wood-framed roofs. From the hundreds of houses built to date, we have learned quite a lot.

THE MATERIAL

Straw

Hay is for horses, and is full of grain and nutrition. *Straw* is the plant structure between the root crown and the grain head, and can be from just about any grass that grows, although agricultural grains are by far the most typical for building. The internal structure of a single straw is tubular, tough, and efficient — it contains cellulose, hemicellulose, lignins, and silica, is springy in bending and high in tensile strength. The tube shape is inherently stable and, with a microscopically waxy coat, slightly hydrophobic. Bales are compressed masses of straw left over after the grain heads are removed. (Modern agriculture is fairly efficient about harvesting the grain, but some grain heads are inevitably left behind. This is potentially of concern to bale builders, in that leftover grain can attract rodents and bacteria and will readily rot if kept moist. In other words, the grain is food to other critters besides us, and you don't want your wall to be edible, so keep those grain heads out of your bales.)

Bales

The straw is raked from the field and fed into mechanical balers —
of which there are at least a half-dozen makes on the market — then
compressed into rectangular blocks that are bound with steel wire or
polypropylene twine. (Some bales are large cylindrical shapes compressed by larger machines, useful for large-scale agriculture but less so
for building.) Bales may be two-string or three-string, from any kind of
grain (in North America, typically wheat, rice, oats, hops, barley, or rye),
and are not homogeneous, i.e., they have some "grain" or orientation —
different qualities in different directions — based on how the baler
works.

The narrow end-faces receive the compression of the baler head,
which thrusts straw masses in "pulses" into the chamber. These pulses,
when compressed, become *flakes* about four inches thick. Thus, a typical

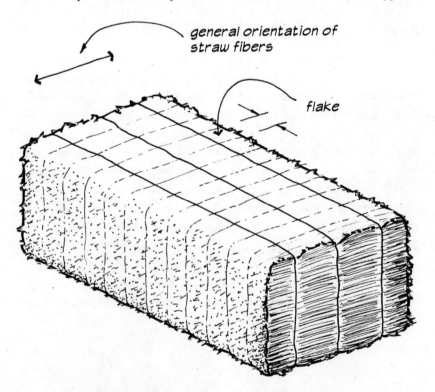

FIGURE 26. *a three-string straw bale*

bale consists of a series of four-inch flakes compressed along the bale's long axis. Because the baler is operating continuously with a series of slightly varying pulses of straw mass, and will only cut and tie off a bale at the end of a flake, bale length will vary by four inches or so.

Bales laid flat — lying on their largest face — carry more load than bales laid on edge (on the other large face). Why? Because simple geometry makes the flat bale more widely based and therefore stronger, but also because the orientation of the straw fibers is predominantly horizontal and therefore more stable. Flat bales are also better for plastering — the exposed cut straw ends are ideal for receiving and bonding to the plaster. Bales laid on edge place the ties (which are now horizontal bands) into tension, which becomes the limit on available edge strength. Furthermore, these ties are exposed along the face of the wall, leaving them more vulnerable to breakage and fire damage (a burst bale, unless it is adequately restrained by surrounding plaster, has no structural value).

Bale Variables

The number of variables in bale production can be maddening; straw bales are almost as far from a standardized building component as they can possibly be. (The same, perhaps even more emphatically, can be said of wood with its many species, grades, shrinkage rates, orientations to grain, etc. But we have the benefit of decades of experience and testing to give us allowable strengths for a huge range of conditions and types of wood.) The different types of straw have varying chemical compositions and inherent strengths, rice straw being perhaps the toughest (and hardest on tools) due to its relatively high silica content.

Moisture content depends on the circumstances at the time of baling and during subsequent storage and transport, but is best kept below 10 to 20 percent (expressed as a percentage of liquid water to the dry bale weight) at time of placement. Bale density varies widely depending on the type of grain, moisture level, and the degree of compression provided by the baler, but should be at least seven pounds per cubic foot (dry density; i.e., with the weight of moisture calculated and subtracted) if intended for use as a load-bearing element.

Even the size of the bales varies with local custom and prevalent balers, although 23 inches wide by 42 to 48 inches long by 15 or 16 inches high is more-or-less standard for three-string bales. Finally, it should be recognized that an erected bale wall will have somewhat different qualities than its component bales because of all the shaving, notching, flake stuffing, and partial bales used to create the desired architectural form.

Considering all this, the difference between any two bales, or any two bale walls, or any two bale structures, can be substantial. Until construction standards are established for straw bales, prudent design must allow for the actual qualities of the specific bales selected for the given project. As a practical matter, specifications must be phrased as performance criteria; e.g., maximum allowable moisture content at time of erection, minimum dimensions and densities, and maximum deflections of wall assemblies under defined, field-simulated loads.

To date, bale builders have generally maintained an attitude of inventive, adaptable practicality in accommodating all the variables associated with straw-bale construction. We have quickly learned that the bales for any project should be purchased in advance, and stored so as to dry out (and preclude the introduction of) unwanted moisture. This

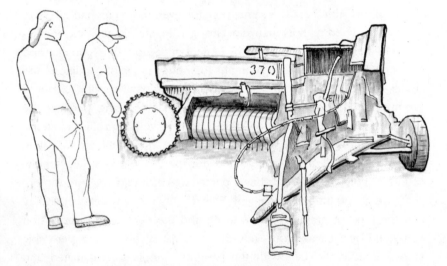

FIGURE 27. *a straw builder, grower, and baler*

also affords a crucial opportunity to measure the bales so as to determine both the density and modular dimensions for design. Even at that, it becomes quickly clear that dimensional tolerances are on the order of several inches as opposed to the +/- 1/4" precision of wood framing. The baler compression should produce dry densities between 7 and 10 pcf (higher density results in only a slight decrease, if any, in insulating value). Although there already exist high-power balers that can doubly compress a standard 46-inch bale down to 23 inches (developed so as to get the maximum amount of material into shipping containers for export), these high-density bales may create more problems than they solve, and their usefulness in construction remains to be explored.

Bale Wall Types

Sometimes called "Nebraska style" because of the historical precedents, load-bearing straw-bale construction denotes construction in which the weight of roofs and floors above the ground are supported, partly or entirely, by the bales. The first load-bearing straw-bale houses were built using simple common sense as a guiding design principle. Common sense still is, and should always remain, the primary guide for any builder, but we also have learned much about how and how not to use straw as a structural building material. It is now possible to benefit from others' experience (and mistakes) and to apply rational analysis to the design of load-bearing straw-bale buildings.

Non-load-bearing denotes construction in which no weight of roofs or floors are supported by the bales; rather, some other type of principal structure carries the loads. The first non-load-bearing straw-bale buildings were agricultural barns, in which the fall grain straw was baled and stacked inside the plank or stone walls, thereby providing insulation through the winter for the livestock. The bales are merely infill between structure, so this category is sometimes also called "straw-bale infill" or "post-and-beam." This type of bale construction has become predominant over load-bearing, as builders oftentimes find it easier, cheaper, and more adaptable, and generally easier for finding acceptance from building inspectors, lenders, and insurers.

Test Results — Straw Bale and Wall Properties

Specific knowledge about the structural strengths of bales and bale walls is available from several testing programs conducted over the past few years, the results of which are summarized in the paragraphs that follow.

■ Bou-Ali tests, Tucson, Arizona

At the University of Arizona in the spring of 1993, in a master's thesis by Ghailene Bou-Ali, both individual bales and unplastered wall assemblies were put through a variety of laboratory trials. The tests used polypropylene 3-string wheat straw bales of dimensions 16" x 23" x 45" and average density of 8.5 pounds per cubic foot.

Tests on individual bales, laid flat, tell us the following:

- The maximum compressive stress increased with bale density, ranged between 70 and 84 psi, and led to a failure vaguely characterized by loss of resistance to the load head (there was no noticeable change in the bale at "failure"; the machine simply registered some loss of resistance and backed off). Most or all deflection rebounded upon removal of load, i.e., "failure load" was still largely within the elastic range of the material. Put more dramatically: a single bale was loaded with 36 tons of pressure, deflected to half of its height, and rebounded within days so as to be indistinguishable from other bales.

- The elastic modulus ranged between 60 and 260 psi, and increased with applied load, i.e., the bales "stiffened up" when compressed.

- Poisson's ratio (the ratio of vertical strain to horizontal strain, or the squish factor over the bulge factor) was 0.3. For example, a bale that loses 10 percent of its height when compressed will gain 3 percent of its length.

Tests on individual bales, laid on edge, tell us:

- The maximum compressive stress was only 17 to 21 psi, and led to a sudden failure (the middle string breaks and the bale partially disintegrates). In other words, the bale capacity is limited by the tensile capacity of the "barrel hoop" strings.
- The elastic modulus ranged between 78 and 211 psi.

Tests on unplastered wall assemblies (12 feet long by 8 feet high, bales flat) tell us:

- Three wall assemblies were tested to 15,800 pounds in compression (4.8 psi), leading to deflections of 6.9, 7.6, and 7.8 inches. The elastic modulus *decreased* with load due to the onset of buckling. (These deflections may be somewhat misleading, both because there was no attempt to pack or press the bales into place, and because the measured deflections are actually the average of the center and end deflections. A well-built wall, with ends braced by crosswalls, will generally compress much less.)
- Three wall assemblies, braced at the tops, were tested for out-of-plane uniform loading (pressure), deflecting at midheight as follows: 3/4 inch @ 20 psf, 1 inch @ 23 psf, and 5/8 inch @ 23 psf. Deflections were greatly reduced (to the stated values) by using four-course-high rebar pins instead of two-course pins.
- Three wall assemblies were loaded at midheight with an in-plane force of 2,135 pounds (or 89 psf of shear), and deflected at the tops as follows: 6 inches, 4.25 inches, and 2.3 inches. The size of the deflections was clearly in inverse proportion to the degree to which nuts at the top of threaded anchor rods (which held down a wooden top plate) were tightened (hand tightened, wrenched, and fully wrench tightened, respectively). In other words, precompressing the wall decreased the in-plane deflection.

■ SHB AGRA tests, Albuquerque, New Mexico

In the fall of 1993, at SHB AGRA laboratories in Albuquerque, plastered and unplastered wall assemblies were subjected to out-of-plane (pressure) loading per ASTM E-330.

Test results on wall assemblies (12 feet long by 8 feet high, bales flat) tell us the following:

- Three unplastered wall assemblies were tested to 20 psf in lateral (out-of-plane) pressure, leading to elastic deflections on the order of 1 inch.
- One plastered wall assembly was tested to 50 psi in lateral (out-of-plane) pressure, leading to an elastic deflection on the order of $1/8$ inch.

These tests show that bale walls are capable of resisting high wind loads with acceptable deflections and that the addition of plastered "skins" enormously increases the wall rigidity. The increase in rigidity, in turn, shows that the wall acts as a structural sandwich panel, with appreciable shear transfer between the skins via the straw. This is discussed further on page 107.

■ Ship Harbour Project tests, Nova Scotia

A two-story, load-bearing studio was built by and for Kim Thompson in 1993, with extensive ongoing testing of thermal, moisture, and structural performance funded by the Canadian Society of Agricultural Engineering.

Individual bales of wheat, barley, and oats were put through laboratory compression tests.

Tests on individual bales laid flat tell us the following:

- The maximum compressive stresses ranged between 6 and 10 psi and led to no failures.
- The elastic modulus ranged between 18 and 26 psi for the various grains. (These comparatively low modulus measurements are perhaps explained by the relatively low loading to which the bales were subjected, i.e., the initial "soft" portion of the stress-strain curve.)

The conclusions of the testers, in their own words, were:

"1. There is considerable variation in the modulus of elasticity between bales of the same type, and [between] bales of a different type.

"2. Bale density has a greater effect on bale strength than bale type. It is perhaps not possible to compact some straw types as tightly as others.

"3. Continuous exposure to high moisture contents decreases the modulus of elasticity.

"4. The Poisson's ratio in the longitudinal direction is much greater than the lateral [sic] in unconfined tests."

■ Fibrehouse Limited tests, Ottawa, Ontario

Architect Linda Chapman and engineer Bob Platts devised (and have applied to patent) a method of precompressing walls using jacks on the wall top plates that grabbed and pulled up 22-gauge chicken wire reinforcing (fastened at the base) on both sides. The tensioned wire fabric gets fastened to the top plate, and the wall is held and plastered in a compressed state. In their report of February 1996, they describe a series of informal laboratory tests for compression and out-of-plane bending on plastered and unplastered assemblies, and the construction of a test structure intended for real use.

Their results clearly show that a precompressed wall (both unplastered and plastered) is enormously stronger and stiffer than its uncompressed counterpart. In compression, the load capacity is improved, largely because initial settling deflections (typically two or three inches for an eight-foot-high wall) have already been taken out. Out-of-plane bending and shear capacities (their tests did not include in-plane shear) are increased as with other precompression systems in construction; the tightly held bale assembly is stronger all around. (By way of analogy, imagine pressing a stack of books onto the floor. The harder you press, the more stable the stack becomes, and the harder it then is to push the stack over from the side.)

Besides providing heightened stiffness, this system also can serve to level the top of the wall and flatten the wall surfaces for plastering, and suggests it may be possible to omit the customary pins between bales. (Under simulated wind pressure of 150 psf, horizontal stucco cracks appeared on the tension face along bale joints, suggesting interbale shear slippage and/or separation. These results demonstrate that an unpinned wall assembly can be quite strong. However, the same test was not performed on a pinned wall for comparison; this might have revealed the shear restraint value of pinning.) The test results also showed high bond between the straw and plaster skins, preventing cracked skins under compressive load from buckling.

ANALYSIS

Load-bearing Straw-bale Walls

The large size of straw bales makes most bale walls inherently sturdy. If you don't try to stack them too high, and/or if you don't have too long a wall without crosswalls, a bale structure will last indefinitely, even in high winds. Recognizing this, codes written to date treat bale walls like masonry, defining limits to the ratios of height (h) to thickness (t), and to the length (l) of unsupported walls. The Pima County, Arizona, straw-bale building code limits h/t to 5.6 (10' 8" high for a 23"-wide wall), and l/t to 13 (25 feet for a 23" wall). The Pima County code further limits total dead plus live vertical loads at the top of a load-bearing straw-bale wall to 360 psf (or 2.5 psi). California's model straw-bale code (adopted by the state legislature — see Appendix S-2 for the complete text) allows an l/t ratio of 15.7 and top-imposed dead plus live loads of 400 psf (or 2.77 psi).

Virtually all straw-bale buildings are *plastered,* where "plastered" is used generically to include traditional mud-based plasters, lime plasters, gunite, cement stucco, and various other high- and low-tech combinations. Cement stucco has known structural properties and therefore is often viewed more receptively by code officials, but, by virtue of being so hard and brittle, it is the most dissimilar to the straw bales. Owners and builders regularly express preference for lime-, mud-, or gypsum-based plasters for their softer look and feel and their qualities of "self-healing" minor cracks, as well as telegraphing subsurface moisture penetration (sounding an alarm before it's too late). But cement stucco remains, for now, the only dependable, quantifiable skin material when structural considerations predominate.

In thinking of plastered, load-bearing straw-bale construction, it is essential to understand that, once plaster is applied directly to either or both bale surfaces, with or without reinforcing mesh, the structure is now a hybrid of straw and plaster. *Effectively, any further loading — snow, people, wind, earthquakes — will go mostly or entirely into the plaster skins.* This is because of relative stiffness, or the relative moduli of elasticity of the two disparate materials. Any kind of plaster is far stiffer than the straw, and will therefore "attract" any subsequent loading. Imagine, for example, walking barefoot across a carpet at night, in the dark, and discovering the sharp-edged little toy your child left there. As you grab your foot and dance around in pain, take an extra moment to reflect on the relative stiffnesses of toys and carpeting, and how your weight all focused on that little, sharp, incompressible truck while the soft carpet all around elastically deflected away from the pressure of your foot.

This suggests what happens when a heavy snow or earthquake comes to visit a plastered load-bearing straw-bale structure. The soft, flexible straw immediately yields, and the brittle plaster skin (effectively a thin concrete wall or very wide, flat column) attracts all the stresses. If not strong enough to carry the new load, it cracks or buckles, unable to elastically deflect or absorb stress. Unlike in a conventional concrete structure, however, where such a failure of a wall or column could be sudden and catastrophic, the failure of the plaster skin will throw any loads back on the straw bale assembly. The capacity of the bales to pick up the load yielded by cracked plaster is unknown, but fairly substantial. The Arizona tests proved that an unplastered wall can carry an appreciable amount of vertical and in-plane shear load and would therefore provide a fairly dependable backup against complete failure of the plaster skins.

The straw bales' usefulness as backup in an earthquake is far less certain. Some bale builders contend that the flexibility of a bale wall makes it ideal for "riding out" dynamic shaking, but the reverse may also be true. The bale assembly might move horizontally and vertically far more than the capacity of the (relatively rigid) roof to stay attached to it, and may also *amplify* seismic ground accelerations like a whip. Without a sturdy, well-designed roof diaphragm and its requisite connections to the walls, there could be a life-threatening danger of roof collapse. We can only speculate as to how big a risk that is: there has been no appreciable dynamic testing of a load-bearing straw-bale wall or structure, in the lab or in the field. (Although plastered load-bearing straw-bale houses have successfully endured moderate earthquakes in Wyoming and the Owens Valley of California, those events were nowhere near the magnitude of the temblors that strike high-risk areas like coastal California.)

Actual building failures and successes, so far, have been largely a matter of trial and error, leaving us with the question of how to rationally design and build a load-bearing straw-bale structure for the expected loads and conditions.

The structural model — the load paths — are complex: rigid inside and outside skins are attached to the comparatively very soft straw-bale "masonry" assembly. The skin material can be known, but the thickness will vary appreciably, and should be assumed to be uniformly the least thickness (e.g., the plaster may vary from one to four inches in thickness as it fills in the gaps and notches). Also, due to the nature of the stacked bales, the skins are never clean, smooth, purely vertical planes. There will always be some slight deviation from plumb, varying in both direction and magnitude. The outside skin is often aligned outside the outer face of both the bearing plate at the top and the foundation; its capacity to resist imposed vertical or shear loads is limited, then, by the capacity of the shear connection between the straw and the plaster. The inside skin usually sits directly on a floor slab, which in turn may or may not be directly over the foundation. The bales themselves are usually pinned and, most importantly to the whole package, there is both some shear capacity in the bales and some shear transfer capacity between the bale surfaces and the skins. Though it is essential to see the plaster skins as the primary load-carrying elements, it is nevertheless also important to recognize that the straw bales are still crucial elements of the package. This is analogous to the relationship of web to flanges in a steel I-beam: the flanges (skins) carry bending loads, but rely on the strong shear capacity of, and connection to, the web (in this case, the straw bale assembly). So the assembly consists of strong, brittle, thin "concrete walls" braced by, and somewhat elastically connected by, the straw bale core. (This type of structure — a "sandwich panel" — is ubiquitous; hollow-core doors and corrugated cardboard are sandwich structures.)

To develop a mathematical model of such a beast, though conceivable, is daunting. And it may not yet be worth the effort: in *assuming* values for each of the many variables, the accuracy of results is incrementally decreased. A theoretical model, then, might yield no useful results or even be dangerously misleading. Even with a level of engineering detailing and field supervision not yet approached in straw-bale construction, the overall behavior of the assembly is virtually untested and unknown, and therefore defies accurate prediction.

Even so, we can and should at least take a cursory look at a plastered straw-bale wall behaving as an integrated sandwich panel. We have a few bits of testing data (albeit far too few and too imprecise to draw any dependable conclusions) that we can use for the exercise.

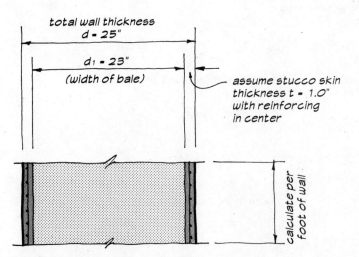

FIGURE 28. *horizontal section through 12-inch length of plastered straw-bale sandwich panel*

The New Mexico transverse load (wind pressure) tests simulated 20 psf of pressure on three unplastered 8' x 12' wall panels using the standards of ASTM E-330. The walls deflected at midheights by 1.87, 0.75, and 1.00 inches, for an average deflection of 1.21 inches. Then, an otherwise identical plastered wall panel was loaded to 20 psf and yielded 0.06 inches, or one-twentieth of the unplastered value (the loading was later increased to 50 psf, where the wall deflection was still only 0.13 inches). The code deflection limitation is 0.5 percent of the height which, for an eight-foot wall, is 0.48 inches. The 8-foot-high by 1-inch-thick cement plaster skins alone have virtually no stiffness, so there is clearly some degree of integrated (sandwich) behavior. (The Ottawa tests also established sandwich panel behavior without quantifying it.)

If the assembly were behaving as a pure sandwich panel, i.e., with minimal shear deflection of the straw bales or straw-plaster boundary, the moment of inertia, per linear foot of wall, would be:

$$I = b \, (d^3 - d_1{}^3) \, / \, 12$$

where:

- $b = 12''$ (a one-foot width)
- $d = 23''$ bale width + (2 x 1.0'' skin thickness) = 25''
- $d_1 = 23''$ bale width

so:

$$I = 12 \; x \; (25^3 - 23^3) \, / \, 12 = 3{,}458 \; in^4 \text{ per ft of wall.}$$

The wall deflection, Δ, under 20 psf of pressure would then be:

$$\Delta = 5wl^4 \, / \, 384 \; E_c \, I_g$$

where:

- $w = 20 / 12 = 1.67$ pounds per inch
- $l = 8' = 96$ inches
- E_c = modulus of elasticity of cement stucco = $57{,}000 \, \sqrt{f'_c}$
  (assume $f'_c = 2{,}500$ psi) $\Rightarrow E_c = 2{,}850{,}000$ psi
- $I_g = 3{,}458 \; in^4$

so:

$$\Delta = 5 \, (1.67) \, (96^4) \, / \, 384 \, (2{,}850{,}000) \, (3{,}458) = 0.0002 \text{ inch}$$

In other words, using the scanty data available, it would seem that a plastered straw-bale wall is 20 times stiffer than its unplastered counterpart (1.21″ / 0.06″), but still about 300 times less stiff than a true sandwich panel (0.06″ / 0.0002″). (Note that this calculation assumes a

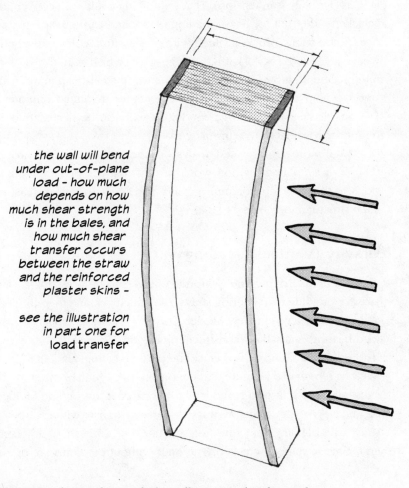

the wall will bend under out-of-plane load - how much depends on how much shear strength is in the bales, and how much shear transfer occurs between the straw and the reinforced plaster skins -

see the illustration in part one for load transfer

FIGURE 29. *plastered straw-bale wall as a sandwich panel*

simple clear span from base to top, where the New Mexico test panels were supported on all four sides. The calculation also ignores shear distortion and bending stiffness of the bales alone, but the imprecision of the available data probably renders any additional calculation accuracy pointless.) As more tests are done to investigate sandwich panel behavior, some usable approximation of wall moment of inertia, such as 1/300 of I_g, should emerge.

Making use of the integrated system will also require designed reinforcing for the plaster skin, which has no tensile strength (the convex skin in Figure 29 is in tension). That reinforcing could be a conventional "chicken wire," but for heavy loading (snow and earthquake) may well need to be some form of welded wire mesh with a comparatively tight weave such as $2'' \times 2''$ with 16-gauge wire (which would give a wall reinforcement ratio of 0.0015 square inches of steel per square inch of stucco, compatible with code requirements for minimum reinforcing). Design and detailing of edge conditions will also be necessary at any boundary considered to transmit loads.

Until more sophisticated analysis of the wall assembly is possible, though, a simplified method would be to treat the plastered skin, or skins, as thin concrete columns or walls, and analyze them as quasi-concrete structural members.

Gravity (Vertical) Loading

The Pima County and California codes provide prescriptive standards for building load-bearing straw-bale structures, and therefore serve as guides. The current New Mexico Code, by contrast, explicitly forbids load-bearing straw-bale construction, largely for fear that the cyclic loading of heavy snows will crack the plaster coating, leading to both a loss of strength and a failure of the moisture protection of the straw-bale substrate, which in turn could lead to moisture intrusion and biological degradation of the structural straw. Experience to date with load-bearing straw-bale buildings in snow country is mixed; some show no distress, and some have been cracked. The ones without problems are presumably, then, ones that have plaster skin structures capable of carrying the loads imposed.

The problem becomes one of calculating the load capacity of the wall skin, or skins. Of key concern are the straightness and the unbraced length, or how "tall," effectively, the plaster wall/column is. This, in turn, begs the question of how regularly along its height the plaster column is braced. Some engineers define adequate bracing as anything that can develop a tensile or compressive restraining force of about 5 percent of the axial force. In other words, if a 12-inch width of the wall is loaded with 500 pounds in compression, restraint is considered to be provided by anything capable of restraining a horizontal force of 5 percent of 500 pounds, or 25 pounds every 12 horizontal inches.

Reports from the field consistently describe how difficult it is to demolish a plastered straw-bale structure, and in particular how hard it is to separate the plaster from the straw, whether hand-applied, troweled, or gunited. This implies that the bonding is uniform and firm, so let us tentatively say that the unbraced height is equal to three times the skin thickness (i.e., that the stucco/straw bond can provide bracing equal to 5 percent of vertical load on a one-inch-thick skin for every three inches of height), and then apply UBC equation 14-1 (in chapter 19) for allowable axial load on a concrete wall:

$$P_{nw} = 0.55 \ \phi \ (f'_c) \ A_g \ [1 - (kl_c / 32h)^2]$$

in which:

- P_{nw} = nominal axial compressive load strength of the wall
- ϕ = strength reduction factor for walls = 0.70
- f'_c = ultimate (breaking) strength of the plaster material
- A_g = gross area of wall/column
- kl_c = factored unbraced length (k is a factor that amends the actual unbraced length, l_c, according to how tightly "held" the top and bottom are)
- h = the wall (i.e., skin) thickness

If we assume kl_c to be equal to 3 x h, then we get:

$P_{nw} = 0.55$ x 0.70 x $(f'_c) \ A_g$ x $[1 - (3/32)^2] = .38 \ (f'_c) \ A_g$

In other words, this suggests that we can use 38 percent of the ultimate compressive strength. Allowing, however, for the irregularities

in the wall surface, and the absence of conventional deformed reinforcing, 10 percent is probably a more prudent figure to use. If the ultimate
strength of the stucco plaster is, for example, 3,000 psi, then the allowable
working compression stress would be 300 psi. This is pretty much
consistent with the UBC allowable shear stress on cement stucco of 180
pounds per foot for 7/8 inches thick (which translates to 206 psi allowable
shear stress). It is also the same (10 percent of f'_c) as the value yielded
using the working stress method of design for allowable compressive

*if there is a load
on the plaster skin...*

*then the straw substrate must be
capable of bracing the skin "column"
in either direction with at least 5% of
that same force, which depends on the
bond between the straw and plaster*

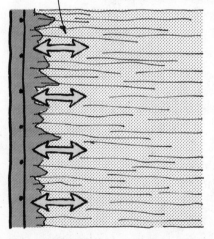

FIGURE 30. *bracing of plastered straw-bale skin*

stress for uninspected reinforced masonry. As a final check, this correlates well with field tests conducted by Dan Smith, Bob Theis, and John Swearingen at the Shenoa Retreat and Learning Center straw-bale cottage in Philo, California. A bale wall with 7/8 inch cement stucco on both sides was loaded for four days, without problem or distress, at 636 pounds per lineal foot (equivalent to 363 psi assuming the load was carried only by the stucco). *We can therefore expect that conventional cement stucco, with good workmanship and wire mesh reinforcing (more than light chicken wire), can be loaded to 10 percent of its ultimate breaking strength in compression. With any other type of plaster, design again becomes a trial-and-error procedure.*

UBC requirements for securing stucco mesh to supporting walls, such as plywood covered with building paper, have unfortunately been transcribed into the first straw-bale codes. Application of the stucco onto bales (worked into the exposed straw fibers) is completely different than stucco applied to plywood or masonry walls (i.e., over a hard, smooth surface), and should be recognized as such. As with other types of construction, stucco netting held tight against the bales serves little purpose. Far more important is the degree to which the first, or scratch, coat of stucco is worked into the exposed straw fibers, establishing the bond between the plaster and substrate (straw). Reinforcing for temperature changes, shrinkage, and structural loading, even if only light stucco mesh, would be far more useful if attached over the scratch coat and under the subsequent coats, or at least held off the surface of the straw, (i.e., in the middle of the plaster skin). In areas of high snow or wind, or *any* earthquake risk, a more substantial reinforcing such as 2x2 16-gauge welded wire mesh would be far better, and should be positively secured to structural boundary elements for load transfer.

Lateral Loading: Wind

The UBC allows cement stucco to be used in limited ways as part of a lateral load-resisting system in frame houses, and plastered load-bearing straw-bale projects to date have shown no problems in resisting wind forces. An 18-foot by 36-foot storage shed built by Tom Luecke in Boulder, Colorado, passed imperturbably through a severe storm with winds in excess of 100 mph; there was no cracking at all. Likewise, the Real Goods Solar Living Center in Hopland, California, was struck in December 1995 with a record windstorm that wreaked havoc up and down California. The building was particularly vulnerable at that time, for there was no glazing on the huge southern walls facing into the storm winds, and the building's shell shape collected and focused winds onto the bale walls (which were coated with a thin gunite substrate and a gunearth facing) on the north side. The walls rode nonchalantly through the tempest without the slightest problem. Finally, load-bearing straw-bale walls in Twila Ard's house in Pensacola, Florida, easily survived a powerful hurricane — before they had been plastered. In short, the empirical evidence to date tells us that straw-bale walls of conventional dimensions are not appreciably affected by high winds.

The Pima County and California code limitations on wall heights, lengths, and openings provide convenient guidelines for empirically designing a plastered load-bearing straw-bale building without actually calculating wind loads. If taller or longer walls or larger openings are desired, attention must be given to the lateral loads that the wall assemblies must carry, and the package designed and constructed accordingly. Again, however, for lack of test information on the behavior of the wall assembly, a dependable structural analysis of load-bearing straw-bale building is limited to designing the cement stucco skins as shear elements, and considering any vertical or shear capacity of the bales to be an unquantified redundancy. For the present, design of unusually shaped load-bearing straw-bale buildings must make use of supplemental, conventional structure to carry part or all of the vertical and lateral loads.

Lateral Loading: Earthquake

Straw-bale designers in California have made use of cement stucco skins, as allowed by the UBC, to carry lateral forces — not without reservations, however, at least on the part of the building inspectors and engineers, for earthquake forces are not kind to brittle things like stucco. Once stucco has cracked, it has lost some or all of its strength, leaving the building vulnerable to aftershocks.

For simpler and smaller load-bearing straw-bale buildings, where calculated stresses are appreciably less than the UBC-allowed 180 plf, no backup system is probably necessary. For the vast majority of building types, however, redundant systems for lateral forces and vertical loads should be built into the system to back up a full or partial plaster failure. Or, lacking certain knowledge about how a plastered load-bearing straw-bale assembly will perform in a large seismic event (or in order to use non-cement plaster), engineers are designing bracing systems to carry 100 percent of earthquake forces. This can be accomplished with light gauge metal straps, tensioned polyester packing straps or heavy wire, or slender threaded bolts set diagonally across the surface of the bale wall and protected by the plaster. The diagonals must be designed for calculated forces, and adequately fastened at the top plate and foundation. Compression struts (such as let-in lumber) may also be necessary at key corners or wall panels to prevent the wall from crushing under overturning forces.

Non-load-bearing Straw-bale Walls

The only structural requirements for non-load-bearing bale assemblies are: to support their own selfweight, and to remain intact under lateral loads. The New Mexico tests on plastered walls impressively demonstrated the walls' capacity to resist out-of-plane (lateral) forces by acting to some degree as a straw/plaster sandwich panel.

The New Mexico straw-bale code addresses non-load-bearing straw-bale construction only (and prohibits load-bearing straw-bale construction), and provides criteria for wall design. It requires that the bales be laid flat, be laid in a staggered (running) bond, and be thoroughly pinned. Walls can be no more than 12 feet high, nor more than 20 feet long between crosswalls. Anchors between bales and surrounding support structure are required at each bale course at vertical sides, and at 24 inches to the horizontal support at the top. Stucco netting (reinforcing) is made optional, while vapor barriers are explicitly forbidden (to let the wall breathe).

The New Mexico code goes on to require the first (scratch) coat of plaster be thoroughly worked into the straw "where stucco netting is not used."

Justification for this phrasing is provided by the adequate performance of unplastered bale walls under out-of-plane loading in the Arizona, New Mexico, and Ottawa tests. The builder is allowed the option of furring the bale surfaces, leaving no contact between plaster and straw.

It is clear, however, that plaster coatings should *always* be worked into the straw unless there is compelling reason not to. The testing showed a huge reduction of deflection from an unplastered to a plastered wall assembly under out-of-plane loading, and the tests and discussion related to load-bearing straw-bale construction clearly show an overall enhancement of the wall performance when the plaster skins are bonded to the straw substrate. Likewise, stucco netting (or, better, welded wire fabric) should always be used, if only for crack control, unless there is a good reason not to. Various methods for weaving, stapling, or tying stucco netting to or through the bale wall have proven labor-intensive, and of varying efficacy (the intent is to prevent large slabs of plaster from peeling away from the wall, particularly during an earthquake). Since the bond provided by working the plaster into the straw is probably far more important for that purpose, many feel that reinforcing need only be attached well enough to stay in place during plastering.

One advantage of non-load-bearing straw-bale construction is the introduced option of stacking the bales on edge, thereby reducing wall thickness. Tests have shown that bales on edge have little load-bearing capacity, but have a higher R-value per inch, so the net thermal insulation of an edge-stacked wall is about the same as a flat-stacked wall. Builders report that plastering is made more difficult because the straw is presented across the face of the exposed wall, as opposed to the end grain exposed in a flat-stacked wall.

The structural system of a non-load-bearing straw-bale wall can be just about anything, and builders have already used 2x braced wood framing, 4-inch or larger timber framing, round pole structures, manufactured wood web joists, site-built plywood box or I-beams, rebar web joists, bamboo web joists, welded steel frames, bar joists, steel studs, and concrete or grouted masonry columns and bond beams. The structural system, in other words, can be anything the local codes allow, and it's worth pointing out that permits are often awarded more readily when the inspector sees a system with which she's familiar. Analysis for vertical and lateral loads is conventional, and the bales must simply be strong enough for their own selfweight, wind pressure on panels, and inertial lateral force of earthquakes.

Another non-load-bearing system, as pioneered by Louis Gagne in Canada, involves laying and mortaring bales in a vertical stacked bond like brick masonry. Horizontal and vertical mortar joints are at least a few inches thick, so the bales are effectively acting as permanent formwork/bracing for a concrete honeycomb structure which bears the loads. As with the earlier discussion regarding rigid plaster skins on soft bale walls, the stiffness dissimilarity of the straw and concrete effectively means that all loads will be carried by the thin concrete webs. For projects of limited size and height, and where little earthquake threat exists, this is a workable system which has been accepted by Canadian building authorities. However, many have questioned the thermal efficiency of this system (because the mortar readily conducts heat), and the required use of so much cement for uncertain benefit. In general, this system has not seen extensive use, and will not be further covered here.

DESIGN AND CONSTRUCTION CONSIDERATIONS

An impressive variety of details for foundations, bracing, precompression, wall openings, and top or cap beams have been tried and/or proposed for straw-bale construction. Many of these have been clearly described and graphically presented in *Build It with Bales* and *The Straw Bale House*, among other publications. I probably could plagiarize all that material or reprint it here, but then you might never go buy or even look at the Bibles of Bale. If you're contemplating building with bales, you should just plain get them. So much of what you need to know is there, as well as many of the things you don't yet know that you need to know.

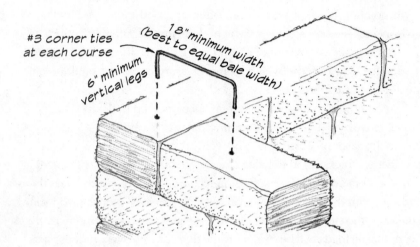

FIGURE 31. *corner pinning*

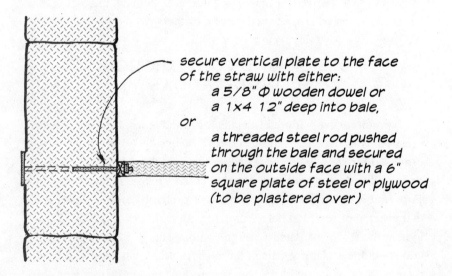

FIGURE 32. *attaching stud walls to straw-bale wall*

Bales and Pinning

Construction quality control begins with the baling of the straw. A well-planned project includes locating the source for the bales, and working with that source to get the optimal "construction grade" bales. Tom Luecke reports that having the bales compressed at night, while the straw is moist and pliable, results in a substantially tighter, more coherent bale because the straw dries in the compressed shape — a quasi-Stramit panel (see Appendix S-1). This probably applies to any straw harvested during hot, dry weather. The reverse is true for crops like rice, which are harvested sopping wet, and must be drained and somewhat dried before baling. In other words, there is an optimal level of moisture/pliability (which differs from one grain to another) that should be reached, either by wetting or drying, as appropriate, before baling. Unfortunately, no specific research has been done to determine this optimal moisture level for the various grains and grasses, so achieving the right level depends on the experience and judgment of the baler.

The sponginess of straw bales makes, unsurprisingly, for some unique onsite construction considerations. Though they are basically stacked like masonry, they don't behave like bricks. Walking along the top of an eight-foot-high, newly stacked bale wall has a slightly Coney Island funhouse feel to it; the wall wobbles, shimmies, and shakes. For this reason, the bales must be pinned during stacking for stability and alignment (or immediately compressed per the Fibrehouse system) and are sometimes braced. Pins are usually steel rebar, which is cheap and easy to drive. However, the steel is enormously stiffer than the surrounding straw, and may therefore be structural overkill. Bamboo or wood dowels are acceptable because they are strong enough that the weakness of the pin joint is still defined by the relatively soft bales; a 3/4-inch-diameter piece of wood or bamboo may even be preferable because it displaces and compacts more surrounding straw, thereby making a tighter joint. Pinning (or omission of pins) is an area needing study. Almost all tests to date have been on pinned walls and the New Mexico, Pima County, and California codes all require extensive pinning with rebar. It is possible, however, that pins make only a marginal structural contribution to a compressed, plastered wall assembly. In other words,

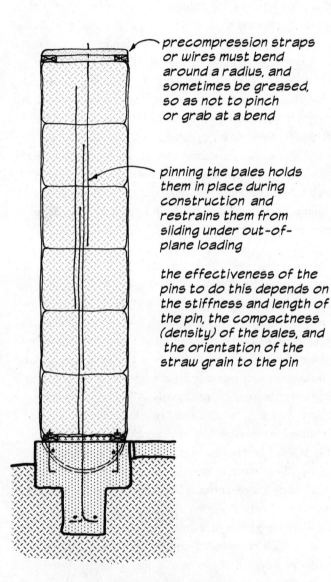

precompression straps
or wires must bend
around a radius, and
sometimes be greased,
so as not to pinch
or grab at a bend

pinning the bales holds
them in place during
construction and
restrains them from
sliding under out-of-
plane loading

the effectiveness of the
pins to do this depends on
the stiffness and length of
the pin, the compactness
(density) of the bales, and
the orientation of the
straw grain to the pin

FIGURE 33. *pinning of straw-bale wall*

the pins may be equivalent to the temporary shoring and bracing that a builder installs during wood-frame erection and, as such, probably should not be prescribed in codes. If this hypothesis should be substantiated by testing, then pinning could and should be considered a jobsite safety issue and left to the builder's discretion.

Wall Settling

A big consideration, also a largely unexplored field of study, is the short-term creep deflection of the bale wall. Straw builders have found that an eight-foot wall can lose one to four inches of height in a few weeks from added roof weight and its own selfweight. They have also found, though, that these deflections are drastically reduced if bales are emphatically stomped both downward and against adjacent bales. (*Stomping* is the best word we can think of — there is no dry, academic engineering term for specifying the proper bale stacking technique. Perhaps someone will think of one, and we will be able to unsqueamishly write construction specifications that don't use words like "stomping," but until then you'd best just get up there and stomp 'em.) Knowing that any appreciable settling of the straw will induce unwanted stresses, and possibly cracks, in the rigid plaster skins that are already in place, homesteaders and modern builders have typically let the loaded walls settle as long as possible before applying plaster.

More recently, however, rather than waiting for the roof weight to compress the bales, some builders have been precompressing the walls mechanically, though sometimes with only partial success. Initially, this was accomplished with all-thread rods every six feet or so beside or through the bales, connecting top plates to foundation, and tightened with nuts at the top. Unfortunately, some precompressed walls were found, a year later, to have settled further on the order of a full inch beneath compression nuts, while others are (so far) performing well.

Tom Luecke pioneered the use of elastic polyester package strapping, and Ted Butchart and Peggy Robinson of Seattle, Washington, have been using agricultural Gripple® clamps with heavy gauge (fencing) wire, in both cases "cinching down" the bale assembly to the foundation at close intervals such as two feet on center. In the similar system described by Linda Chapman and Bob Platts in Ottawa, chicken wire sheets on both faces of the bale wall are grabbed from the top with oak bars, tightened upwards with car jacks pushing down on the top plate, and secured in a taut condition. All of these systems show more promise than the all-thread systems because the tighter spacing allows for some leveling of the wall top by adjusting relative tensions, and because their elasticity (springlike behavior) permits them to maintain some compression on the wall even if it settles. Elastic precompression systems may also render obsolete the need for pinning the bales, as the compressed bale assembly seems to have adequate strength in in-plane and out-of-plane bending and in shear. However, the long-term ability of chicken wire, heavy (agricultural) wire, or polyester strapping to maintain high tension, as well as their use in this type of construction application, is untested and unknown. Anecdotal reports to date are highly positive, but the use of these tensioning systems should be controlled and conservative until there is more of a track record and/or laboratory testing to verify long-term behavior. As a tentative rule of thumb, precompression of the wall should: 1) accomplish initial deflection; i.e., take up the "slack" in the vertical assembly, and 2) at least equal the dead loads that will be subsequently applied before plastering. It should also be noted that some builders use backhoe buckets to press down on the tops of walls while tightening the straps or wire, making the process faster and easier to control. They simply work their way around the perimeter once, and sometimes twice, compressing the wall and leveling the top surface for bearing.

The temptation arises to expect that the tightened bale wall assembly, by being stiffer, will take up any further imposed loads. And, in general, calculations would show that it will have the capacity to do so. But the straw is still far looser (more elastic) than the plaster skins, and so it will remain true that loads applied subsequent to the curing of the plaster skins will be attracted into those skins. Even if the roof bearing assembly is carefully isolated from the skins so as to bear only on straw, deflection of the straw under the bearing surface (even a very slight one) will transfer loads via the adjacent fibers to the surrounding plaster skins.

Precompression has become commonplace as an alternative to letting walls settle over time under dead loads, but the success of the effort is very much dependent on the magnitude of the initial (and sometimes subsequent) compressions, the stiffness and durability of the compressing mechanism and roof bearing assembly (i.e., the extent of creep), and the inherent qualities of the bales. If a precompression stress can be maintained over the long term, the wall will be tighter and less prone to cracking the plaster, and will have enormously more capacity to resist all loads (as was demonstrated in the Arizona and Ottawa tests).

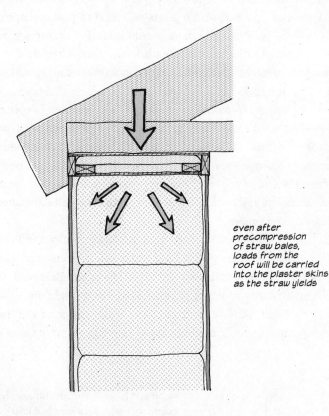

even after precompression of straw bales, loads from the roof will be carried into the plaster skins as the straw yields

FIGURE 34. *top of compressed straw-bale wall under load*

As anecdotal evidence from the growing list of projects keeps coming in, a performance standard that accommodates all these variables will evolve. In the meantime, an engineered load-bearing straw-bale design must include an assessment of the project bales, design and specification of the reinforced plaster skins where loading is large or building geometry unusual, and a defined mechanism and load for precompression (or the willingness to wait for walls to settle for a few weeks under dead load).

Moisture

Water penetration, as with any other type of construction, is a potential problem. Moisture considerations for straw bale walls are very much related to the climate; arid regions will tend to pull moisture out of any wall assembly, whereas warm or cold humidity presents specific vapor problems requiring careful forethought. Straw left in a moist environment will become Black Sticky Goo,[1] not unlike the Gray Mouldy Fluff that framing lumber acquires under the same circumstances. It is generally accepted that avoiding Black Sticky Goo requires keeping the moisture content of a bale wall (expressed as a percentage of water weight to the weight of a thoroughly dried bale) below 15 or 20 percent. This, in turn, gives rise to a host of new questions: Do you need to monitor the moisture? If so, how? And how many points within the mass of the wall need monitoring? Do different grains or cellular materials have different requirements?

While some bale builders are making conscientious efforts to monitor the moisture performance of their walls, most are simply adopting moisture-wary details for the wall construction. Bale walls need to breathe (in the sense of vapor permeability, not outright air leakage) and drain: provision must be made for any water or vapor that might penetrate to escape. (Anecdotal evidence to date suggests that vapor may

1   Black Sticky Goo — in other words, molds and fungi — will flourish anywhere both water and organic matter are present (not just in straw-bale buildings). It is a hazard to the health of your building and, should it become airborne, to you.

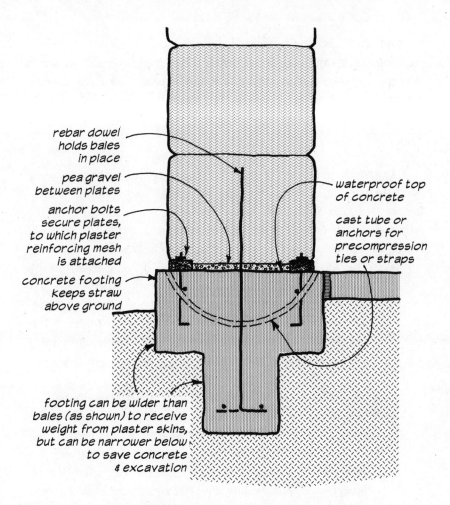

FIGURE 35. *straw-bale wall footing and moisture-proofing*

not be so much of a problem, as outright Black Sticky Goo degradation is only known to have occurred in cases of actual water penetration.) As such, no moisture or vapor barriers are recommended except possibly for the first few courses on the exterior, where rain might splash the wall surface, and on the tops of walls to provide both protection during construction and backup against a roof leak.

The bottom of the wall must emphatically be separated from the foundation; at the very least, a waterproof barrier should be laid over the supporting concrete surface to halt any wicking moisture from below. Additionally, many builders are laying a one-inch layer of pea gravel between 2x4 plates along the inside and outside wall faces, thereby ensuring that the bales will never sit in water.

Fire

In the short history of the straw-bale revival, we have already gathered many stories about fire. This subject is discussed more comprehensively in *The Straw Bale House*, including reference to ASTM fire rating tests done at SHB AGRA labs in Albuquerque. For the purposes of this book, two points deserve mention and emphasis:

- The ASTM tests confirm what we had come to suspect: a plastered straw-bale wall is an excellent fire barrier, possibly deserving as much as a three- or four-hour fire rating. This is simple enough to understand — the bales contain very little oxygen and are too dense to sustain fire. (Imagine trying to burn a telephone book or, better yet, a plastered telephone book, and you will start to get the picture.)

- Emphatically on the other hand, loose straw is *highly* flammable, and loose straw is something that appears in abundance onsite as soon as bales start being cut, shaped, fitted, and set in place. *Any straw-bale construction site, from beginning of bale assembly to cleanup of loose straw (or until plastering, for bales placed on edge with their tie strings exposed and vulnerable), is an extreme fire risk. Extra precautions for fire suppression must be maintained during this period.*

In short, fire is of great concern to the straw-bale builder and of surprisingly little concern to the owner of the finished building.

SAMPLE CALCULATIONS

Note — for simplification, two considerations important to the calculations have been neglected: 1) the added in-plane seismic load from supported crosswalls, and 2) the diminished structural wall length due to window and door openings (see discussion on *piers* in Part One). Although a full, three-dimensional building design would be beyond the scope of this book, any actual building design must account for these and other project-specific factors.

Case 1: Load-bearing Walls

Design a 16-foot by 24-foot, one-story load-bearing cabin for seismic zone 4 (this is an actual project in Parkfield, California, five miles from a very active fault).

The roof is a simple wood-framed shed with light metal roofing. Bales will be locally obtained by the client, a rancher in the area. Available wheat straw bales are 17" x 24" x 48", or 11.33 cubic feet, and weigh 70 pounds each (averaging the measurements of ten individual bales). The density is, then, 70 / 11.33 = 6.2 pcf — *too light* — find others.

Obtain dry oat straw bales 16" x 24" x 48", or 10.6 cubic feet, and weighing 95 pounds each. The density is then 95 / 10.6 = 8.9 pcf — OK.

The walls will then be a multiple of 16" high; use six courses:

$$6 \times 1.33' = 8.0\text{-foot-high wall}$$

■ design for bale bearing and precompression

The roof dead load is 20 psf and the live load is 16 psf. With a two-foot overhang all around, the load tributary to a wall is:

$$(2' + 16'/2) \times (20 + 16) = 10' \times 36 \text{ psf}$$
$$= 360 \text{ plf along top of wall}$$

Provide 14-gauge fencing wire (or wire rated to 500 pounds) tie-downs both sides of wall at 24" oc through foundation and over top plate. Cinch down each wire to 400 pounds (a total of 800 pounds of tension/ precompression every two feet, or 400 pounds per linear foot). The total load on the straw bales is, then, the precompression plus dead plus live loads:

$$= 360 + 400 = 760 \text{ plf}$$

which yields:

$$760/2 \text{ ft. width} = 380 \text{ psf} < 400 \text{ psf}$$

Allowable under California straw-bale code — OK

■ check plaster skin in compression

The roof live load is theoretically all the load that the plaster skins must support, as dead loads are already supported by the compressed bales when the plaster goes on. That (live) load is:

$$(2' + 16'/2) \times 16 \text{ psf} = 160 \text{ plf along top of wall}$$

Because we don't yet know if there will be significant long-term creep in the bales (a "relaxing" of the precompression), it would seem prudent to increase plaster design loads. Let's say, somewhat arbitrarily, that the total load to the plaster could eventually be double the live load, or 320 plf on the assembly, which is 160 plf per skin. We earlier calculated that cement stucco could carry 300 psi in compression, which, for a 1-inch-thick by 12-inch-wide section of wall, is 3,600 pounds per linear foot > 160 — OK

■ design for out-of-plane shear

The walls will be plastered inside and out with conventional three-coat cement stucco using 16-gauge 2" x 2" wire mesh stapled to top and bottom plates with 16-gauge staples @ 12" oc. This system is the same as the assembly tested in New Mexico (see page 102), where a plastered, 8-foot-high wall was loaded to 50 psf and deflected only $^1/_8$ inch at midheight — by inference, the wall is OK for a 20 psf design wind pressure.

■ design for in-plane shear

Calculate the wall's dead weight:

$$\text{Bales: } 2' \times 8.9 \text{ pcf } = 18 \text{ psf}$$

One-inch stucco skins (assume for weight purposes that skins' average thickness is 1.5 inches):

$$(2 \times 1.5" / 12) \text{ cubic feet / sq. ft. } \times 150 \text{ pcf } = 38 \text{ psf}$$

Total wall weight:

$$18 + 38 = 56 \text{ psf}$$

Or, for an 8-foot height, the weight is:

$$56 \times 8 = 448 \text{ plf}$$

The total dead load at the bottom of the wall is:

$$448 \text{ wall weight } + 200 \text{ plf roof load } = 648 \text{ plf}$$

Horizontal earthquake load $F_p = (ZIC_p / R_w) \times W_{DL}$

- $Z = 0.4$ = coefficient for seismic zone 4 (area of highest risk, as in coastal California)
- $I = 1.0$ = coefficient for occupancy importance; higher for hospitals, schools, fire stations, etc.
- $C_p = 2.75$ = structure coefficient for site soil and building structure's response to shaking
- $R_w = 6$ = structure coefficient for type of load-resisting system (in this case, a rigid "concrete" shear wall system)
- $W_{DL} = 648$ plf = the structure dead load

$F_p = (ZIC_p / R_w) \times W_{DL} = 0.18 \ W_{DL} = 119$ lbs/foot

UBC allowable shear load for stucco:

$$F_v = 2 \times 180 \text{ plf} = 360 \text{ plf} > 119 — \text{OK}$$

Secure mesh to straw with 16-gauge wire staples as required and provide spacers as needed to hold mesh 1/2 inch off of straw surface. Install light-gauge galvanized steel diagonal strapping across straw surface (before plastering), fastened securely top and bottom at plates. Provide a minimum of one "X-brace" on each face of building.

Case 2: Non-load-bearing Walls

Design the same walls assuming that the wood framework will support the weight of the roof.

■ design for bale bearing and precompression

The bales must only hold themselves up — OK by inspection.

■ design for out-of-plane shear

The same calculation as above applies; wall panels will be 8 feet high and 8 feet or less wide (post spacing varies with wall openings, but should not be more than two bales, i.e., 8 feet apart).

■ design for in-plane shear

The same calculation as above applies. And, as above, secure mesh to straw with wire staples and provide spacers to hold mesh 1/2 inch off of straw surface. Fasten mesh at vertical posts if exposed to outside of straw. Install steel diagonal strapping, a minimum of one "X-brace" on each face of building.

CONCLUSIONS

Over the past 20 years or so — the infancy of the straw-bale revival — ever-growing numbers of people have been building and experimenting with straw bales as construction materials. There now exists a body of testing and anecdotal knowledge about straw-bale structures that, while modest and inexact, gives us some basis for understanding how these buildings work.

From the outset, we should recognize that we've scarcely begun to explore the potential of the straw bales alone to serve as structural material. As has been discussed, the addition of any plaster to the walls — regardless of whether we can know and quantify the strength — transforms the walls into hybrid straw/plaster bearing elements; the rigid plaster becomes the primary load-carrying element, the straw serves mainly as bracing, and the connection between the two is essential. Yet the tests done to date strongly suggest that straw bales, particularly when pinned and/or compressed, are both an unusual and highly effective weight-bearing material. (The only other materials that can be compressed to half of their height and still be in the elastic range are steel springs and the family of rubber compounds. Maybe someone will start making seismic vibration isolators from bales, for they seem to have all the right qualities.)

Establishing that bales alone can support a roof will, however, be only half the battle. The problem remains of finding construction materials for the rest of the building — not just the plaster skins, but the windows, doors, finishes, roofs — with comparable elastic qualities. A well-built straw-bale wall can probably dance and wave with ease through any snow, wind, or earthquake, showing no permanent distortion after doing so. But it has no dance partner — all the standard materials we use tend to crack or spall or shatter with that much movement. This is no minor matter in a culture with very high expectations of its buildings, and little tolerance for minor defects. We are accustomed to erecting shelter with rigid materials and perfect surfaces, and are unaccustomed, in our thinking about buildings, to a lot of yielding and moving and stretching. (The exception is fabric structures —

tents — so it may be that another architectural vein to be explored is the marriage of straw with fabric. This possibility is made conceivable by the recent development of artificial fabrics that can resist weather, and particularly ultraviolet degradation, for extended periods.)

In any case, the obvious need to plaster straw bales (if only as protection from wear, critters, and moisture) commits us for the time being to thinking of straw-bale construction as *plastered* straw-bale. It is very likely that understanding plastered straw-bale walls as integral sandwich panels will be key to fully exploring the architectural possibilities for this medium. And if someone someday invents a plaster with the right properties of strength, elasticity, permeability, and economy to more closely match the qualities of the straw bales, that will be a wonderful leap forward.

Again, though, we must for the present think of straw-bale buildings as having rigid, brittle plaster skins; effectively, as quasi-concrete structures with very thin, well-braced walls. Pima County or California code guidelines for straw-bale construction should be followed, and load-bearing straw-bale structures should perhaps be limited in size, simple in shape, and not more than one or one-and-a-half stories. Non-load-bearing bale structures are, of course, far less constrained, and structural design of the infill bales simply involves allowing for selfweight and for the lateral pressure on bale panels induced by wind or earthquake (the New Mexico code provides useful guidance here). Load-bearing straw-bale buildings in areas of high snowfall or earthquake risk can be tentatively designed using cement stucco skins (detailed and built for a clear load path from roof to foundation) to carry live loads. Backup (or alternate primary) lateral force systems such as diagonal bracing *must* be built into all but the most simple buildings in seismic zones 3 and 4. Plastered bale buildings never threatened by heavy snow or earthquake are far less problematic, and a wider, less restrictive range of plasters, foundations, and architectural shapes can be perfectly satisfactory.

Precompression of a load-bearing bale assembly, before plastering, clearly has a number of big benefits. At least 2 or 3 psi (288 to 432 psf) of precompression should be designed into the construction sequence (360 psf is the total maximum *imposed* load allowed in the Pima County code, 400 psf in California), and maintained thereafter (in other words, the precompression remains permanently in place). Whatever means is used for compression, such as threaded rods, polyester strapping, or heavy wire, might also be installed diagonally to act as a backup lateral force system.

There remains, of course, quite a long wish list for structural testing. We still know too little about a number of issues:

- The shear capacity of the bales and bale assemblies (plain and precompressed, in-plane and out-of-plane).

- The shear transfer capacity between the straw bales and the plaster skins, i.e., the extent of sandwich panel behavior. Likewise, the tensile bond between the straw and plaster must be established to verify whether or not the tying and stapling of mesh reinforcing currently written into the straw-bale codes is unwarranted (as this author believes).

- The exact effect of precompression on the shear and compressive strengths of the wall and the creep characteristics of long-term loading.

- The exact effect/mechanism of (or need for) pins in the masonry assembly of bales, and the adequacy of pins made of bamboo, reused pipe, wood doweling, or other materials.

- The structural value of any skin material other than cement stucco.

- Potential chemical attack and moisture retention problems (if any) associated with cement plaster on straw.

- The load path for vertical and lateral forces from top plate down to foundation and the effects of combined vertical and lateral loads.

- Appropriate h/t and l/t ratios for stacked, pinned, and precompressed walls.

- The effect of different bale types — grains, moisture levels, densities, preconstruction histories (exposure to weather and critters) — on all of the above.

Having issued these cautious statements, it seems worth noting again — even emphasizing — that there exist many load-bearing straw-bale homes in Nebraska and elsewhere in the West that have peacefully endured more than half a century of snowstorms, high winds, temperature extremes, and human occupancy without ever having had the benefit of rebar pins, precompressing, engineered foundations, and other features that more recently have been deemed crucial. Those houses are out there, uncracked, unrotted, unburnt, possibly as much a testament to the value of common sense in construction and maintenance as to the strength of straw-bale construction. In any case, they're there, and they quietly remind us that straw-bale construction can easily be strong and durable. As a method for engineered design of plastered straw-bale buildings evolves over the years to come, it should continually reflect back on these impressive examples.

APPENDIX S-1: STRAW PANELS

Technologies for manufacturing sturdy, dimensionally stable building panels from straw have slowly evolved over the past few decades and are currently enjoying a noteworthy proliferation. Various forms of straw panels have now been used for interior partitions, finish surfaces, hung ceilings, furniture — and complete modular housing units. As more and more testing is conducted, the surprising structural qualities of these products are emerging.

Unlike all the other materials treated in this text, straw panels are different in that they are both manufactured (as are, to a lesser extent, straw bales and gunned earth) and patentable. As such, there are a variety of products on the market, all of which are proprietary and somewhat unique in their properties. The admittedly cursory review that follows summarizes what structural information I was able to discover about specific products (based on what manufacturers were able and willing to share with me), and then looks at both present and future structural uses for straw panels.

The range of straw panel products can be usefully categorized as:

- Low-density — woven or lightly bound and clearly non-structural, these are strictly for decorative, screening, or light fencing applications.
- Medium-density — extruded without adhesives under heat and pressure, these are dimensionally stable, fairly strong products with a density between 16 and 24 pcf. There are now a number of manufacturers around the world, most using some version of the Stramit manufacturing system developed in Sweden in the 1930s. Already prevalent in Australia and Europe, this type of panel is the most common in the emerging American straw panel industry. The panels usually have some sort of kraft paper facing to receive paint, attached with adhesive, which effectively creates some minor sandwich panel behavior. As with straw bales, the straw is not randomly oriented, so the panels have "grain" — different properties in different directions.

- High-density — bonded with isocyanate adhesives under high heat and pressure and using either chopped straw or longer-length stems, these products are very similar to particleboard and OSB wood fiber panels.

- Sandwich panel — Stramit-type cores bonded to OSB structural facings, these are very strong and promising products. Both because they are not *primarily* straw products and because I was unable to obtain manufacturer's technical data, they are not reviewed here.

A comprehensive review of panel manufacturers has proven virtually impossible, as companies are appearing and disappearing at a brisk rate. A thorough survey in *Environmental Building News* (May/June 1995) is already dated and partially inaccurate, though still an excellent resource. This is a promising and competitive industry still in its infancy, and limited product information is generally available. It generally took repeated and long phone conversations with company owners to obtain testing information, for which I thank them all. (I apologize to those I was unable to reach, but who deserve mention here. Lest anyone wonder, I have no financial relationship with any of the companies mentioned and have tried, with the limited time and resources available to me, to be thorough and impartial.)

Here is a look at four companies' products — three making medium-density panels and one making high-density panels.

Pyramod International, Inc.
City of Industry, California

Envirocor™ panels are medium-density (16-pcf) panels with bonded kraft paper facings, in four-foot widths and thicknesses from 3″ to 4 3/4″. Pyramod is not selling panels, but rather complete modular housing units, having worked out coatings (latex paint) and connections (adhesive and fiberglass tape) for their system. An R value of 1.81 per inch was asserted but not substantiated.

Extensive static and dynamic testing has been performed on individual panels and assemblies. With a simulated dead weight on top, a wall assembly withstood accelerations of 1.0g (i.e., 100 percent of dead load) and exhibited an ability to locally crush or distort so as to absorb excess load without failure (i.e., they showed high ductility). Shear stresses reached 4 psi in-plane, and the compressive elastic modulus was measured at 2,200 psi.

In my conversations with Pyramod president Robert Glassco, he stressed that their product is an entire building package and they have focused their work on developing and testing that package. In so doing, they have come up against the same problem encountered in straw-bale construction: the low elastic modulus makes straw panels structurally incompatible with other, more rigid (or brittle) building materials, particularly in a seismic event. A Pyramod structure can withstand very high wind and earthquake forces and hold up a fairly heavy roof, but cannot always be easily integrated, at least in areas of high seismicity, with other materials such as plaster, tile, wood, or drywall.

Formerly Mansion Industries, Pyramod is one of the first American panel manufacturers.

Stramit, U.S.A. L.L.C.
Perryton, Texas

Note: as of May 1996, Stramit, U.S.A. L.L.C. has closed its doors and is indefinitely out of business. It was, however, the manufacturer by far the most forthcoming and most thorough in providing testing information. I have elected to present some of that information, both in the hopes that Stramit will soon be back in business and with the thought that this data will be inferentially descriptive (to some degree) of Stramit-type panels made by other manufacturers.

Stramit, the company, makes medium-density (24-pcf) Stramit-type panels intended for multiple uses. Production machinery allows for a range of dimensions: the standard panel is 2 1/4″ thick (but can be anywhere from 1″ to 3″) and 4 feet wide; the length is typically 8 feet (but, as the process is a continuous extrusion, lengths can be cut from 3 feet to 12 feet or more). Panels have 85-pound kraft paper bonded to both faces.

Sound absorption, sound transmission, thermal transmission, flame spread, fire resistance, and various structural properties were all tested according to ASTM standards. Selected results of the indicated ASTM tests are summarized below.

■ thermal transmission (ASTM C-518)

R = 2.67 for 2.25" panel

■ nail pull (C-473)

80 lbs — average of five specimens

■ racking load (ASTM E-72)

Results from average of three specimens:
- 1,108 lb failure load (= 5.8 psi in-plane shear for 96" x 2" panels)
- 0.76" deflection @ top (8' ht) @ 790 lb load

■ static pressure (ASTM E-330)

Results from average of three specimens, each 2" x 47" x 94", supported on four sides:
- 116 psf failure load
- 1.048" deflection at middle @ 80 psf

■ impact loading (ASTM E-695)

Results from average of three specimens, each 2" x 47" x 94", supported on two sides:
- a maximum drop height of 54" with a 25-pound bag generated total deflections of 1.71" and permanent deflections of 0.05"

BioFab
Redding, California

Pacific Goldboard panels are medium-density (18 to 20 pcf) Stramit-type panels intended for multiple uses. The standard panel is 2″ or 2 1/4″ x 4 feet x 8 feet. Panels have 69-pound kraft paper bonded to both faces, and an R value of 1.81 per inch was asserted but not substantiated. No structural testing values were available at this writing.

Meadowood
Albany, Oregon

Meadowood makes high-density rye grass panels weighing about 39 pcf and coming in thicknesses from 1/8 inch to 3/4 inch. Unlike the Stramit-type panels, in which heat and pressure alone are used to bond the fibers, Meadowood panels have an isocyanate binder (non-outgassing 30 minutes after manufacture, according to company founder Leonard Opel) to hold the fibers in the dense, hard condition.

The material is hard, stable, and highly resistant to thermal shock, but swells up to 50 percent upon severe exposure to water. A 10-penny galvanized box nail driven into a 1/4″-thick sample 1/4″ from the edge caused no visible distress. Some laboratory testing was done, yielding the results summarized below.

■ **thermal transmission**

R = 0.68 across a 1/4″ specimen
(by inference, the R value would be about 2.7 per inch)

■ **nail pull**

50 lbs — average of 12 paneling (small head) nails of unspecified size

■ **modulus of elasticity**

300,000 psi
(comparable to strong particleboard or lower-grade waferboard)

■ **modulus of rupture**

4,706 psi — average of five specimens tested to failure
(effectively, the ultimate bending strength)

■ **tensile strength**

1,970 psi — average of five specimens

Conclusions

The nascent straw panel industry in the U.S. has to date focused largely on supplying products for non-structural uses such as ceilings, interior partitions, and furniture. No company has yet developed, tested, and marketed a pure straw panel for structural use. Nevertheless, the potential is clearly there for straw panels to be used as shear paneling and light-duty bearing partitions. Pyramod has pioneered the modular straw panel house and others are making stress-skin sandwich panels with medium-density straw cores and OSB skins.

Straw panels in general seem to share both strong and weak traits. They are good sound attenuaters and thermal insulators and have surprisingly good flame spread qualities (product literature is replete with images of smiling workers holding blow-torches against blackened but not burning straw panels.) The panels should gain relatively easy acceptance among builders because they are manufactured to standard dimensions. However, they are readily susceptible to water damage. And, due to their relatively low densities, transportation — of both straw to manufacturing plants and finished panels to end users — is not economical over long distances.

The ideal straw or fiber panel may not yet have been invented; many new products are sure to appear in the years to come. Panels that are being made already, however, will continue to be tested and receive code approvals, and should inevitably become common elements of modern architecture. Though they cannot compete "head to head" with existing engineered wood products, they can nevertheless someday become standard parts of the building designer's palette.

APPENDIX S-2: CALIFORNIA STRAW-BALE CODE

Note: this is reprinted verbatim from the recently enacted legislation. I have used it as a basis to generate specifications for both load-bearing and non-load-bearing straw-bale structures.

Assembly Bill 1314 — Buildings: straw-bale structures.
BILL NUMBER: AB 1314 CHAPTERED 10/16/95

CHAPTER 941

FILED WITH SECRETARY OF STATE OCTOBER 16, 1995

APPROVED BY GOVERNOR OCTOBER 15, 1995

PASSED THE ASSEMBLY SEPTEMBER 12, 1995

INTRODUCED BY Assembly Members Sher, Richter, and Woods (Coauthor: Senator Johannessen)

FEBRUARY 23, 1995

An act to add Chapter 4.5 (commencing with Section 18944.30) to Part 2.5 of Division 13 of the Health and Safety Code, relating to buildings.

LEGISLATIVE COUNSEL'S DIGEST

AB 1314, Sher. Buildings: straw-bale structures.

Existing law, known as the State Building Standards Law, creates the California Building Standards Commission and authorizes it to review proposed building standards, adopt or reject these proposed standards, and codify and publish the adopted standards in the California Building Standards Code. Local agencies have the responsibility for the enforcement of numerous provisions of the California Building Standards Code. This bill would amend the State Building Standards Law to establish safety guidelines for the construction of structures, including single-family dwellings, that use baled rice straw, as defined, as a loadbearing or nonloadbearing material.

This bill would provide that the guidelines proposed by this bill shall not become operative within any city or county unless and until an express finding is made, as specified, and the finding is filed with the Department of Housing and Community Development. This bill would, subject to the availability of funds, require the California Building

Standards Commission, on or before January 1, 2002, to transmit, to the Department of Housing and Community Development and to the Legislature, a report regarding the implementation of the bill.

This bill would specify that none of its provisions be construed as an exemption from either the Architects Practice Act or the Professional Engineers Act, relative to the preparation of plans, drawings, specifications, or calculations under the direct supervision of a licensed architect or registered engineer, for construction of structures that deviate from the conventional framing requirements for wood-frame construction.

SECTION 1. Chapter 4.5 (commencing with Section 18944.30) is added to Part 2.5 of Division 13 of the Health and Safety Code, to read:

CHAPTER 4.5. GUIDELINES FOR STRAW-BALE STRUCTURES

Article 1. General Provisions and Definitions

18944.30. (a) The Legislature finds and declares all of the following:

(1) There is an urgent need for low-cost, energy-efficient housing in California.

(2) The cost of conventional lumber-framed housing has risen due to a shortage of construction-grade lumber.

(3) Rice straw is an annually renewable source of cellulose that can be used as an energy-efficient substitute for stud-framed wall construction.

(4) The state has mandated that the burning of rice straw be prohibited as specified in statute by the year 2000 in an annual phased reduction.

(5) As a result of the mandated burning reduction, growers are experimenting with alternative straw management practices. Various methods of straw incorporation into the soil are the most widely used alternatives. The two most common methods are nonflood incorporation and winter flood incorporation. Economically viable off-farm uses for rice straw are not yet available.

(6) Winter flooding of rice fields encourages the natural decomposition of rice straw and provides valuable waterfowl habitat. According to the Central Valley Habitat Joint Venture component of the North American Waterfowl Management Plan, in California's Central Valley, over 400,000 acres of enhanced agricultural lands are needed to restore

the depleted migratory waterfowl populations of the Pacific flyway. Flooded rice fields are a key and integral part of the successful restoration of historic waterfowl and shorebird populations.

(7) Winter flooding of rice fields provides significant waterfowl habitat benefits and should be especially encouraged in areas where there is minimal potential to impact salmon as a result of surface water diversions.

(8) An economically viable market for rice straw bales could result from the use of rice straw bales in housing construction.

(9) Existing regulatory requirements are costly and severely restrict the development of straw-bale housing.

(10) Statutory guidelines for the use of straw-bale housing would significantly benefit low-cost housing, agriculture, and fisheries in California.

(b) It is therefore the intent of the Legislature to adopt safety guidelines for the construction of structures including, but not limited to, single-family dwellings that use baled rice straw as a loadbearing or nonloadbearing material, provided that these guidelines shall not be effective within any city or county unless and until the legislative body of the city or county makes an express finding that the application of these guidelines within the city or county is reasonably necessary because of local conditions.

18944.31. (a) Notwithstanding any other provision of law, the guidelines established by this chapter shall not become operative within any city or county unless and until the legislative body of the city or county makes an express finding that the application of these guidelines within the city or county is reasonably necessary because of local conditions and the city or county files a copy of that finding with the department.

(b) In adopting ordinances or regulations, a city or county may make any changes or modifications in the guidelines contained in this chapter as it determines are reasonably necessary because of local conditions, provided the city or county files a copy of the changes or modifications and the express findings for the changes or modifications with the department. No change or modification of that type shall become effective or operative for any purpose until the finding and the change or modification has been filed with the department.

18944.32. Nothing in this chapter shall be construed as an exemption from Chapter 3 (commencing with Section 5500) of, or Chapter 7 (commencing with Section 6700) of, Division 3 of the Business and Professions Code relative to preparation of plans, drawings, specifications, or calculations under the direct supervision of a licensed architect or civil engineer, for the construction of structures that deviate from the conventional framing requirements for wood-frame construction.

18944.33. For the purposes of this chapter, the following terms are defined as follows:

(a) "Bales" means rectangular compressed blocks of rice straw, bound by strings or wire.

(b) "Department" means the Department of Housing and Community Development.

(c) "Flakes" means slabs of straw removed from an untied bale. Flakes are used to fill small gaps between the ends of stacked bales.

(d) "Laid flat" refers to stacking bales so that the sides with the largest cross-sectional area are horizontal and the longest dimension of this area is parallel with the wall plane.

(e) "Laid on-edge" refers to stacking bales so that the sides with the largest cross-sectional area are vertical and the longest dimension of this area is horizontal and parallel with the wall plane.

(f) "Straw" means the dry stems of cereal grains left after the seed heads have been removed.

18944.34. (a) Subject to the availability of funds, on or before January 1, 2002, the California Building Standards Commission shall transmit, to the department and to the Legislature, a report regarding the implementation of this chapter.

(b) The implementation report shall describe which cities and counties have utilized this chapter, and the number and type of structures that have been built pursuant to local ordinances. The implementation report may include recommendations to amend the guidelines established by this chapter, or any other related matters.

(c) The California Building Standards Commission may accept and use any funds provided or donated for the purposes of this section.

Article 2. Guidelines for Materials

18944.35. (a) Bales shall be rectangular in shape.

(b) Bales used within a continuous wall shall be of consistent height and width to ensure even distribution of loads within wall systems.

(c) Bales shall be bound with ties of either polypropylene string or baling wire. Bales with broken or loose ties shall not be used unless the broken or loose ties are replaced with ties which restore the original degree of compaction of the bale.

(d) The moisture content of bales, at the time of installation, shall not exceed 20 percent of the total weight of the bale. Moisture content of bales shall be determined through the use of a suitable moisture meter, designed for use with baled rice straw or hay, equipped with a probe of sufficient length to reach the center of the bale, and used to determine the average moisture content of five bales randomly selected from the bales to be used.

(e) Bales in loadbearing walls shall have a minimum calculated dry density of 7.0 pounds per cubic foot. The calculated dry density shall be determined after reducing the actual bale weight by the weight of the moisture content.

(f) Where custom-made partial bales are used, they shall be of the same density, same string or wire tension, and, where possible, use the same number of ties as the standard size bales.

(g) Bales of various types of straw, including wheat, rice, rye, barley, oats, and similar plants, as determined by the building official, shall be acceptable if they meet the minimum requirements of this chapter for density, shape, moisture content, and ties.

Article 3. Construction Guidelines

18944.40. (a) Straw-bale walls, when covered with plaster, drywall, or stucco, shall be deemed to have the equivalent fire resistive rating as wood-frame construction with the same wall-finishing system.

(b) Minimum bale wall thickness shall be 13 inches.

(c) Buildings with loadbearing bale walls shall not exceed one story in height, and the bale portion of the loadbearing walls shall not exceed a height-to-width ratio of 5.6:1 (for example, the maximum height for a wall that is 23 inches thick would be 10 feet 8 inches).

(d) The ratio of unsupported wall length to thickness, for loadbearing walls, shall not exceed 15.7:1 (for example, for a wall that is 23 inches thick, the maximum unsupported length allowed is 30 feet).

(e) The allowable vertical load (live and dead load) on top of loadbearing bale walls shall not exceed 400 pounds per square foot, and the resultant load shall act at the center of the wall. Straw-bale structures shall be designed to withstand all vertical and horizontal loads as specified in the latest edition of the Uniform Building Code.

(f) Foundations shall be sized to accommodate the thickness of the bale wall and the load created by the wall and roof live and dead loads. Foundation or stem walls which support bale walls shall extend to an elevation of not less than 6 inches above adjacent ground at all points. The minimum width of the footing shall be the width of the bale it supports, except that the bales may overhang the exterior edge of the foundation by not more than 3 inches to accommodate rigid perimeter insulation. Footings shall extend a minimum of 12 inches below natural, undisturbed soil, or to the frost line, whichever is lower.

(g) (1) Vertical reinforcing bars with a minimum diameter of 1/2 inch shall be embedded in the foundation to a minimum depth of 7 inches, and shall extend above the foundation by a minimum of 12 inches. These vertical bars shall be located along the center line of the bale wall, spaced not more than 2 feet apart. A vertical bar shall also be located within 1 foot of any opening or corner, except at locations occupied by anchor bolts.

(2) Nonbale walls abutting bale walls shall be attached by means of one or more of the following methods or by means of an acceptable equivalent:

(A) Wooden dowels of 5/8 inch minimum diameter and of sufficient length to provide 12 inches of penetration into the bale, driven through holes bored in the abutting wall stud, and spaced to provide one dowel connection per bale.

(B) Pointed wooden stakes, a minimum of 12 inches in length and 1 1/2 inches by 3 1/2 inches at the exposed end, fully driven into each course of bales, as anchorage points.

(C) Bolted or threaded rod connection of the abutting wall, through the bale wall, to a steel nut and steel or plywood plate washer, a minimum of 6 inches square and a minimum thickness of 3/16 of an inch for steel and 1/2 inch for plywood, in a minimum of three locations.

(3) (A) Loadbearing bale walls shall be anchored to the foundation at intervals of 6 feet or less. There shall be embedded in the foundation a minimum of 2 1/2 inch diameter steel anchor bolts per wall, with one bolt located within 36 inches of each end of each wall. Sections of 1/2 inch diameter threaded rod shall be connected to the anchor bolts, and to each other, by means of threaded coupling nuts, and shall extend through the roof bearing assembly and be fastened with a steel washer and nut.

(B) Bale walls and roof bearing assemblies may be anchored to the foundation by means of other methods which are adequate to resist uplift forces resulting from the design wind load. There shall be a minimum of two points of anchorage per wall, spaced not more than 6 feet apart, with one located within 36 inches of each end of each wall.

(C) With loadbearing bale walls, the dead load of the roof and ceiling systems will produce vertical compression of the walls. Regardless of the anchoring system used to attach the roof bearing assembly to the foundation, prior to installation of wall finish materials, the nuts, straps, or cables shall be retightened to compensate for this compression.

(h) (1) A moisture barrier shall be used between the top of the foundation and the bottom of the bale wall to prevent moisture from migrating through the foundation so as to come into contact with the bottom course of bales. This barrier shall consist of one of the following:

(A) Cementitious waterproof coating.

(B) Type 30 asphalt felt over an asphalt emulsion.

(C) Sheet metal flashing, sealed at joints.

(D) Another building moisture barrier, as approved by the building official.

(2) All penetrations through the moisture barrier, as well as all joints in the barrier, shall be sealed with asphalt, caulking, or an approved sealant.

(i) (1) For nonloadbearing walls, bales may be laid either flat or on-edge. Bales in loadbearing bale walls shall be laid flat and be stacked in a running bond, where possible, with each bale overlapping the two bales beneath it. Overlaps shall be a minimum of 12 inches. Gaps between the ends of bales which are less than 6 inches in width may be filled by an untied flake inserted snugly into the gap.

(2) The first course of bales shall be laid by impaling the bales on the rebar verticals and threaded rods, if any, extending from the foundation. When the fourth course has been laid, vertical #4 rebar pins, or an acceptable equivalent, long enough to extend through all four courses, shall be driven down through the bales, two in each bale, located so that they do not pass through the space between the ends of any two bales. The layout of these rebar pins shall approximate the layout of the rebar pins extending from the foundation. As each subsequent course is laid, two pins, long enough to extend through that course and the three courses immediately below it, shall be driven down through each bale. This pinning method shall be continued to the top of the wall. In walls seven or eight courses high, pinning at the fifth course may be eliminated.

(3) Alternative pinning method: when the third course has been laid, vertical #4 rebar pins, or an acceptable equivalent, long enough to extend through all three courses, shall be driven down through the bales, two in each bale, located so that they do not pass through the space between the ends of any two bales.

The layout of these rebar pins shall approximate the layout of the rebar pins extending from the foundation. As each subsequent course is laid, two pins, long enough to extend through that course and the two courses immediately below it, shall be driven down through each bale. This pinning method shall be continued to the top of the wall.

(4) Only full-length bales shall be used at corners of loadbearing bale-walls.

(5) Vertical #4 rebar pins, or an acceptable alternative, shall be located within one foot of all corners or door openings.

(6) Staples, made of #3 or larger rebar formed into a "U" shape, a minimum of 18 inches long with two 6-inch legs, shall be used at all corners of every course, driven with one leg into the top of each abutting corner bale.

(j) (1) All loadbearing bale walls shall have a roof bearing assembly at the top of the walls to bear the roof load and to provide the means of connecting the roof structure to the foundation. The roof bearing assembly shall be continuous along the tops of loadbearing bale walls.

(2) An acceptable roof bearing assembly option consists of two double 2-inch by 6-inch, or larger, horizontal top plates, one located at the inner edge of the wall and the other at the outer edge. Connecting the two doubled top plates, and located horizontally and perpendicular to the length of the wall, shall be 2-inch by 6-inch cross members, spaced no more than 72 inches center to center, and as required to align with the threaded rods extending from the anchor bolts in the foundation. The double 2-inch by 6-inch top plates shall be face-nailed with 16d nails staggered at 16-inch o.c., with laps and intersections face-nailed with four 16d nails. The cross members shall be face-nailed to the top plates with four 16d nails at each end.

Corner connections shall include overlaps nailed as above or an acceptable equivalent, such as plywood gussets or metal plates. Alternatives to this roof bearing assembly option shall provide equal or greater vertical rigidity and provide horizontal rigidity equivalent to a continuous double 2 by 4 top plate.

(3) The connection of roof framing members to the roof plate shall comply with the appropriate sections of the California Building Code.

(k) All openings in loadbearing bale walls shall be a minimum of one full bale length from any outside corner, unless exceptions are approved by an engineer or architect licensed by the state to practice. Wall or roof load present above any opening shall be carried, or transferred, to the bales below by one of the following:

(1) A frame, such as a structural window or door frame.

(2) A lintel, such as an angle-iron cradle, wooden beam, or wooden box beam. Lintels shall be at least twice as long as the opening is wide and extend a minimum of 24 inches beyond either side of the opening. Lintels shall be centered over openings.

(3) A roof bearing assembly designed to act as a rigid beam over the opening.

(l) (1) All weather-exposed bale walls shall be protected from water damage. However, nonbreathing moisture barriers shall not be used on the upper two-thirds of vertical exterior surfaces of bale walls in order to allow natural transpiration of moisture from the bales.

(2) Bale walls shall have special moisture protection provided at all window sills. Unless protected by a roof, the tops of walls shall also be protected. This moisture protection shall consist of a waterproof membrane, such as asphalt-impregnated felt paper, polyethylene sheeting, or other moisture barrier, as approved by the building official, installed in a manner that will prevent water from entering the wall system at windowsills or at the tops of walls.

(m) (1) Interior and exterior surfaces of bale walls shall be protected from mechanical damage, flame, animals, and prolonged exposure to water. Bale walls adjacent to bath and shower enclosures shall be protected by a moisture barrier.

(2) Cement stucco shall be reinforced with galvanized woven wire stucco netting or an equivalent, as approved by the building official. The reinforcement shall be secured by attachment through the wall at a maximum spacing of 24 inches horizontally and 16 inches vertically.

(3) Where bales abut other materials, the plaster or stucco shall be reinforced with galvanized expanded metal lath, or an acceptable equivalent, extending a minimum of 6 inches onto the bales.

(4) Earthen and lime-based plasters may be applied directly onto bale walls without reinforcement, except where applied over materials other than straw.

(n) (1) All wiring within or on bale walls shall meet all provisions of the California Electrical Code. Type "NM" or "UF" cable may be used, or wiring may be run in metallic or nonmetallic conduit systems.

(2) Electrical boxes shall be securely attached to wooden stakes driven a minimum of 12 inches into the bales, or an acceptable equivalent.

(o) Water or gas pipes within bale walls shall be encased in a continuous pipe sleeve to prevent leakage within the wall. Where pipes are mounted on bale walls, they shall be isolated from the bales by a moisture barrier.

REFERENCES

General

Appropriate Building Materials, Roland Stulz and Kiran Mukerji, SKAT/Intermediate Technology Publications, St. Gallen, Switzerland/London, UK, 3rd revised edition, 1993

Earthword, the Journal of Environmental and Social Responsibility, issue no. 5, 1994, EOS Institute, Laguna Beach, CA

Engineering within Ecological Constraints, National Academy of Engineering, edited by Peter C. Schulze, National Academy Press, Washington, D.C., 1996

Fundamentals of Reinforced Masonry Design, Ajit Virdee, S.E., Concrete Masonry Association of California and Nevada, 1988

"Northridge Earthquake: Lessons Learned," May 18, 1994, Seminar Notes, Structural Engineers Association of Northern California

Shelter, Shelter Publications, Bolinas, CA, 1973

Straw Bale Construction and the Building Codes: A Working Paper, David Eisenberg (unpublished), Version 1.5, 1996

Timber Reduced Energy Efficient Houses, Ed Paschich and Paula Hendricks, Sunstone Press, Santa Fe, 1994

The Tire House Book, Ed Paschich and Paula Hendricks, Sunstone Press, Santa Fe, 1995

1994 Uniform Building Code, International Conference of Building Officials, Whittier, CA, May 1, 1994

Stabilized Earth

ACI Manual of Standard Practice, American Concrete Institute, Detroit, Michigan, 1994

Adobe and Rammed Earth Buildings, Paul McHenry Jr., John Wiley & Sons/University of Arizona Press, Tucson, 1984

Building in Cob, Pisé, and Stabilized Earth, C. Williams-Ellis, John and Elizabeth Eastwick-Field, Country Life Ltd., London, 1947

Dwelling on Earth, David Easton, self-published w/o date, Napa, CA

Earth Construction, a Comprehensive Guide, Hugo Houben and Hubert
    Guillaud, Intermediate Technology Publications, London, 1989

The Earthbuilder's Encyclopedia, Joseph Tibbets, Southwest Solaradobe
    School, Bosque, New Mexico, 1989

PCA Soil Primer, Portland Cement Association, Skokie, Illinois, 1992

Properties and Uses of Cement-Modified Soil, Portland Cement Associa-
    tion, Skokie, Illinois, 1992

The Rammed Earth House, David Easton, Chelsea Green Publishing,
    White River Junction, Vermont, 1996

Soil-Cement Construction Handbook, Portland Cement Association,
    Skokie, Illinois, 1995

"State of the Art Report on Soil Cement," Report of ACI Committee 230,
    American Concrete Institute, Detroit, Michigan, 1990

Straw

*Most of the publications below can be obtained from Out-On-
Bale by Mail, 1039 East Linden, Tucson, AZ 85719.*

Build It with Bales, Matts Myhrman and Steve MacDonald, self-published,
    v. 1.0, Tucson, Arizona, 1995

"Cement-Bonded Straw Slabs: A Feasibility Study," Lars-Anders Hermans-
    son, *Building Issues,* vol. 5, no. 2, 1993

*Developing and Proof-Testing the "Prestressed Nebraska" Method for
    Improved Production of Baled Fibre Housing,* Fibrehouse, Ltd. with
    Scanada Consultants Ltd., Ottawa, Ontario, February 1996

Environmental Building News, May/June 1995, West River Communica-
    tions, Brattleboro, Vermont

House of Straw: Straw Bale Construction Comes of Age, U. S. Department
    of Energy Publication, April 1995

The Last Straw, quarterly newsletter from Out on Bale (Un)Ltd., Tucson,
    Arizona

Meadowood Industries, Inc., Albany, Oregon — product literature,
    results from US Testing Laboratories

Plastered Straw Bale Construction, David Bainbridge with Athena and
    Bill Steen, self-published, 1992

Pyramod International, Inc., City of Industry, CA — product literature; "Experimental Results of Compressed Straw Panels for a Novel Modular Construction System," Marvin Halling, John Krowas, and John Hall, California Institute of Technology, Pasadena, CA (undated); "Structural Behavior of Pyramod™ Structures using Envirocor™ Paneling," J. B. Hoerner and Associates, 1990

Stramit U.S.A. L.L.C., Perryton, Texas — product literature, results from AGRA Testing Laboratories, Albuquerque, NM

Straw Bale Construction — A Manual for Maritime Regions, Straw House Herbals/Solterre Design, Ship Harbour, Nova Scotia (undated)

The Straw Bale House, Athena Swentzell Steen, Bill Steen, David Bainbridge, with David Eisenberg, Chelsea Green Publishing, White River Junction, Vermont, 1996

Straw Bales and Straw Bale Wall Systems, Ghailene Bou-Ali, master's thesis at University of Arizona, Tucson, 1993

Strawbale@crest.org, Internet listserver

Thermal and Mechanical Properties of Straw Bales As They Relate to a Straw House, Canadian Society of Agricultural Engineering, Ottawa, Ontario, 1995

SEISMIC ZONE MAP OF THE UNITED STATES

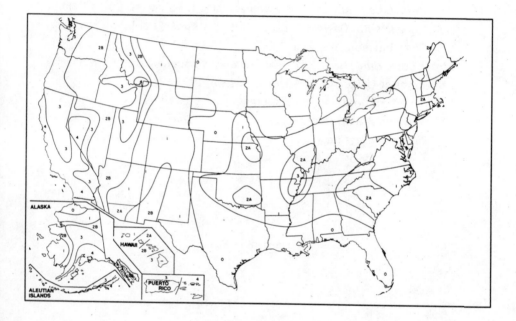

(reprinted from the 1994 Uniform Building Code)

UNIT CONVERSION TABLES

SI SYMBOLS AND PREFIXES

Base Units

Quantity	Unit	Symbol
Length	Meter	m
Mass	Kilogram	kg
Time	Second	s

SI Prefixes

Multiplication factor	Prefix	Symbol
$1,000,000 = 10^6$	mega	M
$1,000 = 10^3$	kilo	k
$100 = 10^2$	hecto	h
$10 = 10^1$	deka	da
$0.1 = 10^{-1}$	deci	d
$0.01 = 10^{-2}$	centi	c
$0.001 = 10^{-3}$	milli	m

SI Derived Units with Special Names

Quantity	Unit	Symbol	Formula
Frequency (of a periodic phenomenon)	hertz	Hz	$1/s$
Force	newton	N	$kg\text{-}m/s^2$
Pressure, stress	pascal	Pa	N/m^2
Energy, work, quantity of heat	joule	J	$N\text{-}m$
Power, radiant flux	watt	W	J/s

Conversion Factors

To convert	to	multiply by
LENGTH		
1 mile (U.S. statute)	km	1.609 344
1 yd	m	0.9144
1 ft	m	0.3048
	mm	304.8
1 in	mm	25.4
AREA		
1 mile^2 (U.S. statute)	km^2	2.589 998
1 acre (U.S. survey)	ha	0.404 6873
	m^2	4046.873
1 yd^2	m^2	0.836 1274
1 ft^2	m^2	0.092 903 04
1 in^2	mm^2	645.16
VOLUME, MODULUS OF SECTION		
1 acre ft	m^3	1233.489
1 yd^3	m^3	0.764 5549
100 board ft	m^3	0.235 9737
1 ft^3	m^3	0.028 316 85
	L(dm^3)	28.3168
1 in^3	mm^3	16 387.06
	mL (cm^3)	16.3871
1 barrel (42 U.S. gallons)	m^3	0.158 9873
(FLUID) CAPACITY		
1 gal (U.S. liquid)*	L**	3.785 412
1 qt (U.S. liquid)	mL	946.3529
1 pt (U.S. liquid)	mL	473.1765
1 fl oz (U.S.)	mL	29.5735
1 gal (U.S. liquid)	m^3	0.003 785 412

* 1 gallon (UK) approx 1.2 gal (U.S.)

** 1 liter approx 0.001 cubic meters

To convert	to	multiply by
SECOND MOMENT OF AREA		
1 in^4	mm^4	416 231 4
	m^4	416 231 4 x 10^{-7}
PLANE ANGLE		
1° (degree)	rad	0.017 453 29
	mrad	17.453 29
1' (minute)	urad	290.8882
1" (second)	urad	4.848 137
VELOCITY, SPEED		
1 ft/s	m/s	0.3048
1 mile/h	km/h	1.609 344
	m/s	0.447 04
VOLUME RATE OF FLOW		
1 ft^3/s	m^3/s	0.028 316 85
1 ft^3/min	L/s	0.471 9474
1 gal/min	L/s	0.063 0902
1 gal/min	m^3/min	0.0038
1 gal/h	mL/s	1.051 50
1 million gal/d	L/s	43.8126
1 acre ft/s	m^3/s	1233.49
TEMPERATURE INTERVAL		
1°F.	$^\circ$C. or K	0.555 556
$^5/_9 ^\circ$C. = $^5/_9$K		
EQUIVALENT TEMPERATURE (t_oC. = TK - 273.15)		
t_oF.	t_oC.	t_oF. = $^9/_5 t_o$C. + 32
MASS		
1 ton (short***)	metric ton	0.907 185
	kg	907.1847
lb	kg	0.453 5924
1 oz	g	28.349 52
*** 1 long ton (2,240 lb)	kg	1016.047

To convert	to	multiply by
MASS PER UNIT AREA		
1 lb/ft^2	kg/m^2	4.882 428
1 oz/yd^2	g/m^2	33.905 75
1 oz/ft^2	g/m^2	305.1517
DENSITY (MASS PER UNIT VOLUME)		
1 lb/ft^3	kg/m^3	16.01846
1 lb/yd^3	kg/m^3	0.593 2764
1 ton/yd^3	t/m^3	1.186 553
FORCE		
1 tonf (ton-force)	kN	8.896 44
1 kip (1,000 lbf)	kN	4.448 22
1 lbf (pound-force)	N	4.448 22
MOMENT OF FORCE, TORQUE		
1 lbf-ft	N-m	1.355 818
1 lbf-in	N-m	0.112 9848
1 tonf-ft	kN-m	2.711 64
1 kip-ft	kN-m	1.355 82
FORCE PER UNIT LENGTH		
1 lbf/ft	N/m	14.5939
1 lbf/in	N/m	175.1268
1 tonf/ft	kN/m	29.1878
PRESSURE, STRESS, MODULUS OF ELASTICITY **(FORCE PER UNIT AREA) (1 PA = 1 N/m^2)**		
1 tonf/in^2	Mpa	13.7895
1 tonf/ft^2	kPa	95.7605
1 kip/in^2	Mpa	6.894 757
1 lbf/in^2	kPa	6.894 757
1 lbf/ft^2	Pa	47.8803
Atmosphere	kPa	101.3250
1 inch mercury	kPa	3.376 85
1 foot (water column at 32°F.)	kPa	2.988 98

To convert	to	multiply by
WORK, ENERGY, HEAT (1J = 1N-m = 1W-s)		
1 kWh (550 ft-lbf/s)	MJ	3.6
1 Btu (Int. Table)	kJ	1.055 056
	J	1055.056
1 ft-lbf	J	1.355 818

INDEX

Bruce King *studied buildings and structures at the University of Colorado, where he earned a degree in architectural engineering. He has worked on the structural design of highrise office towers, hospitals, Polynesian resorts, aircraft, and hundreds of houses,and was introduced to both earth and straw construction while working on the Real Goods Solar Living Center in Hopland, California. He now lives with his family by the shore of the San Francisco Bay, where he has a structural engineering consulting business.*

Buildings of Earth and Straw *was designed and typeset by Ann V. Edminster, design AVEnues, Pacifica, California.*

Printed on 100 percent recycled (50 percent post-consumer) paper. Cover printed with soy-based inks.